Exploring Theory
with
PRACTICA MUSICA™

Exploring Theory
with
PRACTICA MUSICA™

Jeffrey Evans

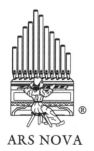

ARS NOVA

Editor   Patricia Carbon

Cover: Steven Brown, Santa Barbara Artworks

© 1999, 2000 by Ars Nova Software. All rights reserved.

First Edition, revised 9/00

03 02 01 00 9 8 7 6 5 4 3

Some material in this book previously appeared in *Windows on Music*, © 1989, 1994 by Ars Nova Software.
All music examples created with Ars Nova's *Songworks II* and exported with Songworks' *Take a Picture* feature.
Practica Musica and *Songworks* are trademarks of Ars Nova Software.

ISBN 0-929444-08-6
Printed in the United States of America

Table of Contents

Preface   ix
Introduction   x

I. NOTATION OF PITCH   **1**
   The Half Step and Whole Step   1
   Octaves and Pitch Class   2
   Solmization (solfège)   2
     Movable do and Fixed do   3
     Writing Pitches with Solmization Syllables 3
   The Staff and its Clefs   3
   Reading Pitches in the Common Clefs   4
   Ledger Lines   5
   Notating a Melody in the Treble Clef Staff 6
   Writing Music by Hand   6
   The C Clef   7
   The Octava G Clef   7
   Origins of the Black Keys   7
   Using Accidentals   8
   Enharmonic Equivalents   9
   Diatonic vs. Chromatic   9
   Summary   10

II. NOTATION OF RHYTHM   **11**
   The Beat and the Measure   11
   The Symbols of Rhythm Notation   12
     Beams   12
     Dotted Notes   13
     Rests   13
  Meter   14
     Simple Meter   14
     Duple and Triple Meter   15
     Compound Meter   15

   Beaming with a Purpose   16
     Beaming in 6/8 and 3/4   17
   Stem and Flag Direction   17
   Asymmetrical Meter   18
   Keeping Notation Simple   19
   Summary   20

III. READING RHYTHM   **21**
   Vocalizing the Beat   21
   Mental Conducting   22
   More on Metric Accents   23
   Beyond the Written Note   25
   Summary   27

IV. COMPLEX RHYTHM   **28**
   The Tie   28
   Syncopation   28
   Hemiola   29
   Triplets, Duplets, and Tuplets   30
   Summary   31

V. INTERVALS   **32**
   Naming Intervals   32
   Major and Minor Intervals   32
   Perfect Intervals   33
   Augmented and Diminished Intervals   33
   Interval Chart   33
   Beyond Augmented and Diminished   34
   Identifying Intervals Quickly   34

WORKSHEETS (tear-out)

Preface

This text is meant to accompany the computer program *Practica Musica*™, version 4. Practica Musica provides a wealth of practical exercises, and this book makes much use of the software to find the reality behind the abstractions of pitch, harmony, and rhythm. Practica Musica supports the text in many ways: it supplies audio accompaniment to each chapter by playing all the music examples; its *Textbook Activities* coordinate with chapters of the book; students can use the software to identify chords and intervals, to hear complex rhythms, and as a general ear training tutor. They can even apply the knowledge gained in the text to write and print their own music.

The subject matter covered in the text is that of an introductory music theory course, though some chapters will at times go well beyond the essentials of an introduction. Similarly, the software has something for both beginners and more advanced students: the higher levels of play in each activity can be challenging to anyone, while the correction capabilities and friendly patience of the computer should help even the shyest novice. The variety of instructional approaches can only grow, since the new software allows instructors to create activities on their own. Ars Nova is supplying diverse activities on the enclosed CD and at the Ars Nova web site (www.ars-nova.com). We hope that professors will add their own creations to this library of instruction.

Much of the text is taken from the Third Edition of *Windows on Music,* but we have reorganized and extended the material. We have also devised a collection of special Practica Musica activities that are coordinated with the text and particularly appropriate for the beginning music student or non-major (the program also includes more difficult activities). The *Textbook Activities* cover most of the material that is normally tested in the form of written exercises, with the advantage of providing instant feedback and individual progress reports. But you will also find here written exercises that give the student experience in putting music on paper. Certain tasks, after all, are best done by hand — for reasons both practical and aesthetic.

We have added a group of rounds for class singing, a tuning-up exercise, and a rhythm band page, on the theory that if students are able to practice their basic skills with the computer there will be more time in class for those things a computer can't do, which include both discussion with the instructor and group activities such as singing in parts.

Belated thanks are due the school where I did my graduate work, the University of California at Santa Barbara; it was there in 1986 that the first version of Practica Musica was written, with the aid of a grant from the Office of Instructional Development. And particularly I would like to express my thanks to all those professors and music instructors who have written over the years either with corrections or with new ideas for the text and the software. Both are better for it.

Introduction

The object of our study is the musical language developed in Europe over the course of the last 1000 years, particularly the tonal music that is associated with such composers as Bach, Mozart and Beethoven and which also forms the basis of modern popular music.

What we want to learn first about this language of sound is its notation — how to read it and how to write down what we hear or imagine in a way that can be easily understood by others.

Along the way to musical literacy we'll gain some insights into how tonal music came to be, and we'll acquire familiarity with its basic materials: the *beat,* the *measure, major* and *minor scales,* and *triads.* We'll study the way that the basic materials of music are built into melody and harmony, and describe principles that can help you to write music of your own. If you take an interest in traditional music of other cultures, or in western jazz or contemporary music, you will find that this knowledge retains its usefulness.

I. NOTATION OF PITCH

The two basic elements of music are *pitch* and *rhythm*. "Pitch" refers to the highness or lowness of a note. "Rhythm" refers to the pattern in time made by a series of notes. Standard music notation provides a simple way to represent both pitch and rhythm.

To understand pitch notation it will help to understand the concept of the *scale*, a set of pitches arranged in a pattern of small and large musical steps. There are various types of scales, each of which follows its own pattern. Standard pitch notation and the white keys of a piano keyboard both evolved to represent the pattern of large and small steps contained in the notes A,B,C,D,E,F,G. When those notes are played starting with C, the pattern is called the *major scale*, the scale of much familiar music.

The Half Step and Whole Step

The small and large steps that form the major scale pattern are called the *half step* and the *whole step*. A half step is the smallest distance between two keys on the piano; a whole step is equal to two half steps. The best way to explain these is to let you hear them.

 Launch Practica Musica and open the Textbook Activity called *1.1. The Keyboard*. Click the mouse cursor on the piano key labeled C, and slide it to D. The difference in sound between those two is a whole step. Now play D, E. Another whole step. But what about E, F? Though the keys appear to be the same distance apart, the sound difference between E and F is a half step. Can you find the other white keys that are a half step apart?

The piano's white keys contain two half steps: E-F and B-C. As you have probably noticed, there is no black key between white keys a half step apart, since a half step is the smallest step possible on a piano.

 Once you've familiarized yourself with the sounds of the half step and whole step, test your ability to tell the difference between them with Textbook Activity *1.2. Whole Step - Half Step*.

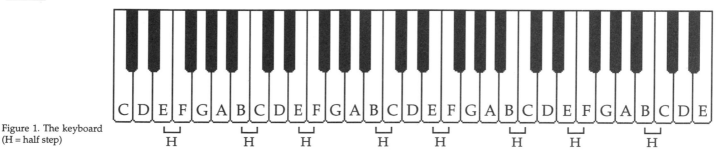

Figure 1. The keyboard
(H = half step)

Octaves and Pitch Class

You can see in figure 1 that the white keys of the piano create a pattern of seven letters, A through G, in alphabetical order. From any starting point, the pattern will begin again at the eighth note, which is an octave away from where you started (*octo* = eight). The octave of any note sounds like a higher or lower version of the same pitch, so we give it the same letter name.

Musicians say notes that are octaves of each other, such as the Fs or the Gs, have the same *pitch class*. The keyboard's white keys really include only seven pitch classes, and all the others are octaves of those seven. This should make your task of learning music seem much easier: a piano may have fifty-two white keys, but they are just the same seven pitch classes repeated in different octaves.

All our scales continue as far as the octave of their starting note and then they repeat. You could say that *a scale is a pattern of steps for filling in the space of an octave.*

Select Practica Musica's Textbook Activity *1.1. The Keyboard* again. Begin on any C and play the piano's white keys in ascending order. Can you hear the pattern begin again on the eighth note? Now listen to the sound of two notes that are an octave apart (notes with the same letter name). Can you hear the difference between notes that are octaves of each other and two notes with different letter names?

The Textbook Activity *1.3. Octaves* will test you on your ability to recognize the sound of octaves.

Solmization (solfège)

The major scale consists of this pattern of whole and half steps: W, W, H, W, W, W, H. A good way to remember the major scale pattern is to practice singing it with the *solmization* syllables *do, re, mi, fa, sol, la, ti,* pronounced "dough, ray, mee, fah, soul, lah, tea" (sometimes *si* is used instead of *ti*).

C D E F G A B C
do re mi fa sol la ti do

In the C major scale (the major scale that begins on C), *do* is C, *re* is D, *mi* is E, and so on. So the half steps E-F and B-C use the syllables *mi-fa* and *ti-do*. Since the word "scale" comes from the Latin word for "ladder " you could visualize the scale steps as unequal rungs on a ladder, as shown at right.

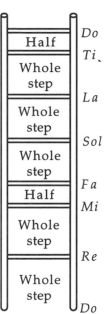

Figure 2. The major scale

Moveable Do and Fixed Do

In this book the syllable *do* will always represent the first note of a major scale, a system that is called *moveable do*. So if we start a major scale on E then E would be called *do*. In France and Italy *fixed do* is traditional; in that system the note C is always called *do*, even if it is not the first note of the current scale. Each system has its advantages, but you'll find that the moveable *do* system makes it easier for you to sing the major scale starting on any pitch.

Writing Pitches With Solmization Syllables

Most popular melodies can be played on the white keys of the piano, since they usually consist of no more than the seven notes of a single major scale. That makes it possible to write the pitches of a melody just with letters or solmization syllables, like this:

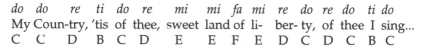

Figure 3. Notating a melody with solmization syllables or letters

The melody so far consists of five pitches: *ti, do, re, mi,* and *fa* in the major scale that starts on C. Very few well-known tunes include more than seven pitches, and many have less, so you could use letters or syllables as a type of music notation. Solmization syllables would be best, since they are the same for any starting note. However, writing this way is awkward, and it doesn't tell you the octave of the scale notes referred to, and it doesn't show the rhythm of the tune. *Staff notation* is both more graceful and more informative.

The Staff and its Clefs

The whole note

Staff notation has evolved over the last thousand years to a form that is very efficient for tonal music. It is based on the idea of writing note symbols on a group of horizontal lines that represent the scale. The vertical position of a note identifies the pitch — a higher position means a higher pitch—and the shape of each note tells the rhythm. For now we'll use only one note shape, the *whole note*.

The staff used today has five lines (originally it was just one and for a while it was four), and notes can be drawn either on a line or on the space between two lines. The lines and spaces refer to the same notes as the white keys of the keyboard, and a *clef* sign is placed at the beginning of the staff to indicate which lines are which.

The most common *clefs* are the G clef, 𝄞, and the F clef, 𝄢, usually presented in the *treble* and *bass* positions. *Clef* comes from the French word for "key," and you can see that it does act as a key to understanding the staff notation: the G clef circles the line representing the G above "middle C" (the C that is midway between the two clefs) and the two dots of the F clef mark the line taken by the F below middle C. Often the treble and bass staves are used together in a combination known as the *grand staff* (left).

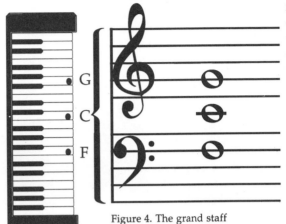

Figure 4. The grand staff

Remember that the lines and spaces of the staff correspond to the white keys of the piano! If you move to the next line or space you move to the next white key and the next letter name, the sound of which can be either a whole step or a half step higher. For example, from the second line of a treble clef to its second space is the whole step G-A. But the distance from the third line to the third space is the half step B-C:

G -A (whole step)   B - C (half step)

 Figure 5. Whole step and half step

Reading Pitches in the Common Clefs

Students of music often use mnemonic devices to remember which staff notes are which in the bass and treble clefs. For example, "**FACE**" and "**All Cows Eat Grass**" remind you of the notes for the spaces in the treble and bass clefs. "**Every Good Bird Does Fly**" can be used for the lines of the treble clef, and a similar device is illustrated at right for the lines of the bass clef. If you forget these mnemonics just remember that the treble clef circles G and the bass clef points to F, and that every line and space represents a letter in ascending alphabetical order from A through G. But the time will soon come when you recognize each pitch without thinking about it.

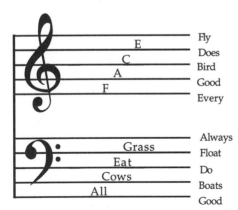

Figure 6. Remembering the staff pitches

Launch the Textbook Activities *1.4. Reading Treble Clef* and *1.5 Reading Bass Clef* for practice in reading the notation of the pitches represented by the white keys of the piano. All you have to do in these exercises is to play the piano key that corresponds to each note in the staff. Rhythm and speed don't matter in this case; just find the notes. If you'd like more practice later, try the first level of Pitch Reading in the standard Practica Musica activities—that exercise rewards you for speed as well as for accuracy.

Ledger Lines

What if you want to write a pitch that is higher or lower than the staff's five lines allow? You could change to a different clef (see below), but in most cases it is simpler to add a *ledger line* (sometimes spelled *leger*), which is an extension of the staff system. To write a note that is higher or lower than the limits of the staff you add more lines, but you make them short — just a little wider than the note, like this:

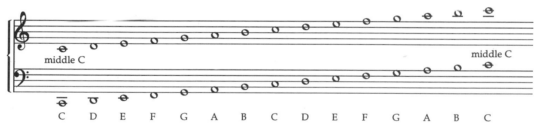

Figure 7. Ledger lines

The first C below the treble clef staff is called "middle C" because it is between the treble and bass clefs, but middle C is also approximately in the center of a full-size piano. Middle C has one ledger line, whether it is written descending from the treble clef staff or ascending from the bass clef staff.

Ledger lines provide a good way to extend the reach of the staff without making it much harder to read (the alternative would be to add more lines to the staff, which might confuse the eye). You'll find that notes written with several ledger lines quickly become familiar.

Notating a Melody in the Treble Clef Staff

If we ignore rhythm, we can now put the melody of "My Country, 'tis of Thee" into staff notation. Listen to Practica Musica play the music in figure 8 (Textbook Activities, Examples, Chapter 1) and follow along as the corresponding piano keys highlight.

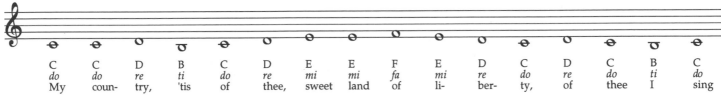

C	C	D	B	C	D	E	E	F	E	D	C	D	C	B	C
do	*do*	*re*	*ti*	*do*	*re*	*mi*	*mi*	*fa*	*mi*	*re*	*do*	*re*	*do*	*ti*	*do*
My	coun-	try,	'tis	of	thee,	sweet	land	of	li-	ber-	ty,	of	thee	I	sing

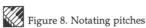 Figure 8. Notating pitches

Writing Music by Hand

Even though computers can do an excellent job of printing music there will be many times when you will need to be able to write it by hand. This skill is particularly useful if you happen to think of a nice musical idea at a time when all you have to work with is a paper and pencil. There's also a certain pleasure to be found in writing music by hand, which you can discover as you gain skill. Finally, writing musical exercises by hand is a good way to help you learn the material.

Remember that everyone has an individual style of handwriting, and yet the symbols need to be easily recognizable by others. Your first efforts at writing should be made with great care to follow a model; later you can go more quickly and you'll find that your own style will develop naturally. You can practice on the staff paper at the end of this book, beginning with the treble and bass clefs.

Figure 10. Handwriting by Bach, Mozart, and Beethoven

Figure 9. Drawing the treble and bass clefs

The C Clef

The C clef points to middle C, and can be placed on any of the five lines of the staff, reducing the need for ledger lines. In its alto position it is the traditional clef used in music for the viola. The tenor C clef is sometimes found in music for the cello, bassoon, or trombone. The soprano, mezzo, and baritone positions of the C clef are mostly of historical interest today. Here are all the C clefs, each followed by a whole note on middle C:

alto   tenor   soprano   mezzo   baritone

Figure 11. Various positions of the C clef

The Octava G Clef

The G clef can be drawn with an 8 below it to indicate that it is an octave lower than its normal treble position. This variation makes a convenient substitute for the alto or tenor C clefs, and is often used in their place in modern music. It covers almost the same range as the alto and tenor clefs, but can be easily read by anyone who knows the treble clef. In the illustration at right it is followed by a whole note on middle C:

Figure 12. Middle C in the octava G clef

Origins of the Black Keys

Early keyboards — those made about the same time that solmization was invented — had only white keys, since they were designed to play a limited pattern of scale steps that corresponds to the notes we use today for the C major scale.

But if your keyboard has only white keys, what happens if you want to play the major scale starting on some note other than C? This would be called *transposing* the major scale pattern. If you have only the white keys to work with you'll run into trouble on the step between your third and fourth notes (A and B) — it will make a whole step instead of the required half step. But you can fix your keyboard by adding another key whose pitch is midway between A and B. Then the major scale on F can be played as below:

Since the fourth note of the scale was going to be named B we will say that this lowered version is still a kind of B: it is "B flat," a B played a half step lower than its unaltered form. In fact, this was the first black key to be added to the keyboard, and that's how the flat symbol came to resemble a small "b": early composers wrote the

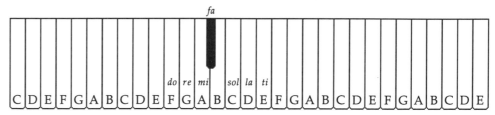

Figure 13. Playing the F major scale

higher form of B (the one on the white key) with square edges (♮) and the lower form with rounded edges (♭). They called the higher form "hard" (B *durum*) while the lower one played on the black key was "soft" (B *molle*). You may recognize the "hard B" symbol as the precursor of the modern *natural* sign (♮) which is now used to indicate a note played in its unaltered form, on the white keys. Another descendant of the former "hard B" sign is the *sharp* (♯) which is used for notes that are *raised* a half step.

Soon black keys were added to fill in every whole step on the keyboard; they allow you to play major or minor scales or melodies beginning on any note you choose. The black keys ended up grouped in threes and twos because the original white keyboard had half steps between E and F and between B and C — a black key was unnecessary in those places.

Using Accidentals

The signs for the sharp and flat are placed before the note they affect, on the same line or space as the note head, and when placed this way are called *accidentals*, though of course they are actually put there on purpose. A sharp (♯) before a note raises it a half step; a flat (♭) means to lower it by a half step. In most cases a sharp or flat will put you on a black key, but not always. Notice, for example, that a "C ♭" will be played on the same key as B (since B is a half step lower than C). The natural sign (♮) reminds you that a note is to be played in its natural form, on the white key that bears its name. There are times when you need to sharp a note that is already sharped, while keeping the same letter name, or to flat a note that is already flat. For those unusual cases we have the double sharp (𝄪) and the double flat (♭♭), which raise and lower a note by two half steps.

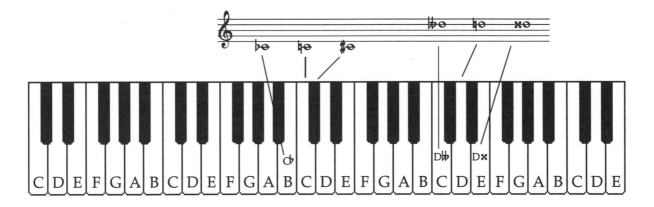

Figure 14. Flatted or sharped notes are not always played on black keys

Enharmonic Equivalents

The names of the black keys vary according to how you're using them: the one between F and G, for example, may be called "F sharp"(F♯), an F raised one half step, or it may be called "G flat" (G♭), a G lowered one half step. In fact, any of the piano's keys can have different names.

Figure 15. Some enharmonic equivalents

How do you know which name to use for a note that can have several? It depends on the context of the melody and harmony. If you are playing a melody based on the major scale starting on D, the third note of the scale must be some kind of F. (Remember that scale steps follow the alphabet.) Since the third note needs to be played a half step higher than the natural F, we name it F♯. G♭ would sound the same on a piano, but G♭ doesn't belong in the D major scale, and using it would imply things that you probably don't intend. F♯ and G♭ are examples of *enharmonic equivalents* — pitches that have different names but which are played on the same piano key. In theory, enharmonic equivalents are not exactly the same pitch, but for convenience we tune the piano so that the same key can play both.

Diatonic vs. Chromatic

You will sometimes need to know the difference between the *diatonic* half step and the *chromatic* half step. The diatonic half step is the one found in the major scale; it is always spelled with a change in letter name, such as E to F, or A to B♭. The chromatic half step is one in which the letter name stays the same, such as C to C♯, or B♭ to B natural. Although C to C♯ and C to D♭ look like the same half step on the piano, the difference in spelling has different musical implications. See page 36 for more on the subject of enharmonic equivalents.

Reading the pitches gets harder now that a note can be altered by accidentals. This is the time to open the Textbook Activities folder again and choose *1.6. Reading Accidentals*. When you hear a round of applause it means you understand the material so far and have graduated from the activity.

Summary, Chapter I

1. The two basic elements of music are *pitch* and *rhythm*.

2. The basic units of pitch are the *half step* and the *whole step*, patterns of which form our common scales, such as the major scale.

3. The *major scale* can be seen as a repeating pattern of whole (W) and half (H) steps: W W H W W W H. The piano's white keys C, D, E, F, G, A, B, C follow this pattern.

4. Notes with the same letter name are *octaves* of each other and have a similar sound. Such notes are said to have the same *pitch class*: all the Cs on the piano have the same pitch class, though they are different in octave.

5. The *solmization* syllables *Do, Re, Mi, Fa, Sol, La, Ti* are a traditional way of memorizing the sound of the major scale pattern.

6. Most well-known melodies are limited to the notes of a single scale, such as the major scale.

7. Pitches are notated on a five-line *staff* whose lines and spaces correspond to the major scale pattern, which also matches the white keys of the piano.

8. The *clefs* drawn on a staff tell which lines or spaces are which. The *treble G clef* circles the note G above middle C, the *bass F clef* marks the note F below middle C.

9. *Ledger* (or *leger*) lines are short extensions of the staff that are used to write notes that go above or below the range of the current clef.

10. The *C clefs* mark middle C; the most common C clefs are the alto C clef and the tenor C clef.

11. The *octava G clef* is a treble clef with an "8" below; it marks a G one octave lower than that of the treble clef, and makes a good substitute for the alto and tenor C clefs.

12. *Sharps* (♯) and *flats* (♭) are used to raise or lower the pitch of a note by one half step. A *natural* sign (♮) means to play the note in its unaltered form, corresponding to a white key on the piano. Sharps and flats make it possible to play a given scale beginning on any note.

13. Sharps and flats are not necessarily black keys: for example, the piano key used to play B natural can also be called "C flat."

14. *Enharmonic equivalents* are pitches that have different names but are played on the same piano key.

15. A *diatonic* half step is one whose letter name changes, such as A to B♭. A *chromatic* half step repeats the same letter, as in A to A♯.

II. NOTATION OF RHYTHM

The Beat and the Measure

If you were inventing your own system of writing music, how would you indicate *when* each note should be played and *how long* it should last?

Modern rhythm notation defines a rhythm by relating it to a steady pulse, real or imaginary, called the *beat*. For example, some notes may last two beats, some one beat, some only one half beat or less. The beats themselves are counted evenly, like the ticking of a clock, and they are counted in groups called *measures* or *bars*. The measures are usually of two, three, or four beats, and they might sound like this if you were to count them out loud:

2-beat measures: "One two One two One two One two "

3-beat measures: "One two three One two three One two three"

4-beat measures: "One two three four One two three four"

The larger letters represent *metric accents*. A note played on an accented beat is often slightly louder or longer than others, or is emphasized in some other way. Usually the first beat of any measure will have the strongest accent, which is called the *primary accent*. Later we'll see that some measures also have a weaker *secondary accent*. For example, 4-beat measures can have a secondary accent on the third beat, like this:

"One two three four One two three four"

Measures are separated in notation by vertical *bar lines*. Special forms of the bar line are used to mark endings and repeats. The repeat signs, though, are not true bar lines since they do not necessarily mark the beginning or end of a measure.

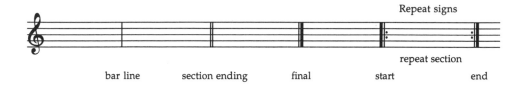

Figure 1. Bar lines

The Symbols of Rhythm Notation

All the symbols for musical notes are derived from the basic one we have already been using, which is called the *whole note*.

A note half as long as a whole note is called, of course, a *half note*, and it is made by adding a *stem* to the whole note:

Figure 2. Several whole notes separated by bar lines.

Figure 3. One whole note is worth two half notes.

Then we fill in the half note to make a *quarter note*, equal in time to one-fourth of a whole note, add a *flag* to make an *eighth note*, and then add more and more flags as needed; two flags for a *sixteenth note*, for example. In theory we could keep adding flags forever and make shorter and shorter notes, but you will rarely see a note shorter than a sixty-fourth, which has four flags.

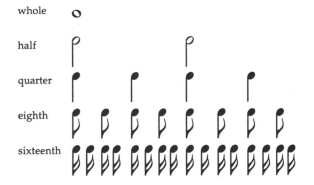

Figure 4. Tree of note values

Beams

Beams are a substitute for flags. You can beam together two or more notes that would otherwise have flags as long as there aren't any unbeamed notes separating them. The number of beams equals the number of flags for each note value.

Figure 5. Beamed notes

Dotted Notes

A *dot* lengthens a note by half its value. For example, since a quarter note is equal to two eighth notes, a dotted quarter note will be equal to three eighth notes. The dotted note often appears as part of a *dotted pair*, in which it is combined with a short note equal to one-third of its value. Usually the dotted note comes first, as in figure 6. An additional dot adds half the value of the previous one, making the more unusual *double dot*.

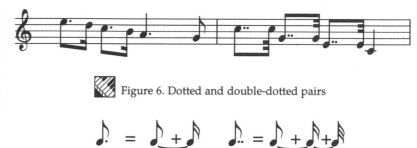

Figure 6. Dotted and double-dotted pairs

Figure 7. Table of notes and their equivalent rests

Rests

A *rest* indicates a length of silence. For every note value there is a corresponding rest, as in figure 7. The difference in appearance between the whole rest and the half rest is hard to remember at first. Perhaps it will help if we say that the whole rest symbol fills the top half of a space to show that it has greater value than the half rest, which fills the lower half of a space. Some people remember by saying that the *half* rest looks like a *hat*:

Though rests are silent you don't just skip over them! The beat continues at a steady pace through a measure of rests just as it would with notes.

Figure 8. Try listening to this example in Practica Musica, and watch the beat marker.

Meter

So far we have discussed only relative note values: we know that a half note is half as long as a whole note, for example, but we don't know how many beats to count for either of them. That information is provided by the *meter signature*, also called the *time signature*, which appears at the beginning of the piece, right after the clef and the *key signature*, which we'll discuss in chapter 6. Unlike the clef and key signature, which repeat on every line of music, a meter signature appears only once at the beginning of a piece and at any change of meter.

Figure 9. Meter signatures 3/4, 4/4, 4/8

There are two basic types of meter: *simple* and *compound*, and their signatures are interpreted differently.

Simple Meter

In the case of simple meter, the upper number specifies the beats per measure while the lower number tells which note value gets one beat. The upper number can be anything, but the lower number is limited to those that represent note values and usually is 2 (half note), 4 (quarter note), or 8 (eighth note). A "4/4" signature tells the reader that each measure of the following music will have four beats and that the quarter note will count as one beat. It doesn't mean that every measure will necessarily have four actual quarter notes in it — only that the value of the notes in the measure will add up to equal four quarters. For instance, a measure of 4/4 might contain two half notes, or three quarters and two eighths, or a single whole note. And if one quarter note equals one beat in 4/4 time then an eighth note will last half a beat, a half note will last two beats, a whole note four beats, and so on.

4/4 is probably the most frequent meter in classical and popular music; it is sometimes called *common time*. Another you will often see is 2/2, or *cut time*, which allows the same number of quarter notes in each measure as 4/4 but counts only two beats per bar, so that the half notes each get one beat. For this reason cut time (sometimes called *alla breve*) is often used for fast pieces. In cut time an eighth note lasts only a quarter of a beat, a quarter note is half a beat, and a whole note is worth two beats.

Often the meter signature for 4/4 is written not with numbers but with the sign, **C**, which means the same thing. A **¢** is used to represent 2/2 (4/4 "cut in half"). You can listen to this example in Practica Musica to hear how the meaning of the half note changes in cut time:

 Figure 10. Common and cut time (4/4 and 2/2)

Duple and Triple Meter

That " **C** " meter signature in figure 10 does not stand for "common" — it is a remnant of the earliest rhythmic notation. It was originally not a letter C, but a half-circle, and it was used to signify a meter that, in modern terms, had a measure divisible by two, which we now call a *duple* meter. A full circle referred to a meter equivalent to what we now call a *triple* meter: divisible by three.

3/4 is a familiar simple triple meter: each measure has three beats, and the beat is counted in quarter notes with the accent falling on the first beat of each measure. You can easily recognize the 3/4 meter of waltz music:

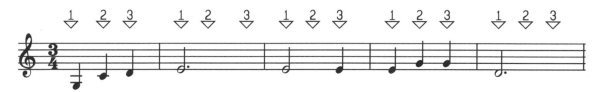

 Figure 11. 3/4 meter in a waltz melody

Compound Meter

Simple meters are those in which the beat is counted by an undotted note, which can be divided in halves. In *compound* meters the beat is represented by a dotted note, which of course divides in three. If 6/8 were a simple meter you would count six beats to the measure, each the value of an eighth note. But music in 6/8 most often has a quick tempo, in which case musicians count only two beats to the measure, each the value of a dotted quarter (three eighths). The meter signature for a compound meter would be more logical if it had a dot beside the lower number and listed the actual performed beats per measure above it (e.g., $\frac{2}{4}$.instead of $\frac{6}{8}$), but traditional practices are not always logical.

Other meters usually performed as compound are 3/8, 9/8 and 12/8, with one, three, and four beats to the bar, respectively. This familiar childrens' melody should give you the feel of a compound 6/8:

The   it- sey bit- sey   spi-   der   ran   up   the wa- ter   spout,

 Figure 12. Compound meter

How can you tell if a meter is compound? It depends both on how the music is written and how it is performed. If the notes of each measure are grouped in threes, with each group being fast enough to count as a single beat, then the meter is compound. One giveaway is the sight of a dotted note that is followed by another dotted note instead of being part of a "dotted pair." That may imply that the beat is moving with the dotted notes, as in this example of a compound 9/4:

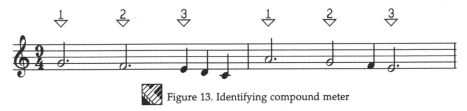

 Figure 13. Identifying compound meter

Figure 16 (see below) presents another example of the difference in appearance between simple and compound meters.

Beaming with a purpose

Now that you know the importance of the beat in rhythm notation you can appreciate that beams are best used to group notes together to make the beats clear to the eye of the reader. Figure 14 has several examples of flagged notes that are beamed together to make plain the start of a beat:

Figure 14. Easy-to-read rhythmic notation

The notation in figure 15 would sound the same as the above example if played by a computer, but it makes little sense visually and would make very hard reading for a human:

Figure 15. The same rhythm, but hard to read

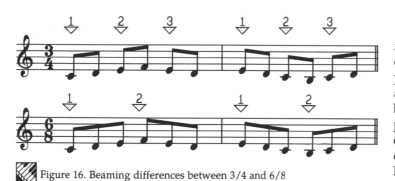

Beaming in 6/8 and 3/4

 Figure 16. Beaming differences between 3/4 and 6/8

Music in 6/8, if beamed incorrectly, may look like it's really in 3/4. In 6/8 performed with two beats to the bar you must be careful to beam your eighth notes in threes instead of twos, unless you are deliberately making a special effect. Otherwise you could accidentally give the impression of three beats to the bar. Incorrect beaming could cause a musician to confuse the performance by putting the accents in the wrong places. The examples at left have exactly the same notes and note values, but they would sound different if well-performed. Try listening to this example using Practica Musica (see also page 25).

 Practica Musica's Textbook Activity *2.1. Meter Examples* will present you with a number of examples of music in different meters, just for listening.

To practice what you've learned about note values and meter, try Textbook Activity *2.2. Placing Bar Lines*. The examples you'll see are beamed for the given meter, but the measure lines are missing and need to be placed in the correct positions.

Stem and Flag Direction

Stems can go either up or down. Either way the note will sound the same, but the choice of stem direction may be important for visual clarity. If you have only one line of music on a staff then the stem direction depends on position; notes above the middle of the staff have their stems down and those on the middle line or below have their stems up. *Remember that descending stems are always on the left side of the note head and ascending ones are always on the right. Flags, however, always wave to the right (the wind blows from the start of the music!).*

 Figure 17. Stem direction has no effect on the sound

Figure 18. Using stem direction to separate voices (From J.S. Bach, "Ein' feste Burg")

Sometimes composers writing music with several parts on one staff use stem direction to show that certain notes follow each other or are performed by the same voice or other instrument. In that case they will ignore the rule about staff position and just make one part's notes all with upward stems and another all with downward stems. In this music for soprano, alto, tenor, and bass, the soprano's notes have upward stems, the alto's downward, the tenor upward again, and the bass downward.

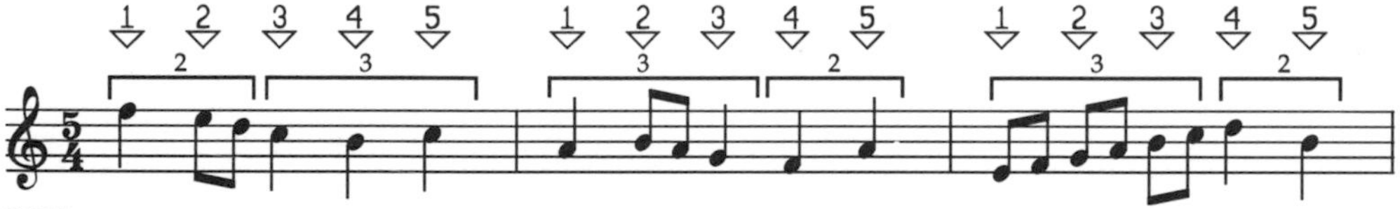

Asymmetrical Meter

All of the meters discussed so far are symmetrical in that their beats per measure can be evenly divided either by two (4/4, compound 6/8) or three (3/4, compound 9/8). That is, they are either duple or triple meters. On occasion you'll encounter music written in an *asymmetrical* meter whose beats per measure do not divide evenly by either three or two, such as 5/4 or 7/4 or 7/8. Such meters have often been used in our own century by both "serious" and pop musicians. Familiar examples are Dave Brubeck's *Take Five*, in 5/4 time, and the Beatles' *All you need is love*, much of which is in 7/4.

Figure 19. An example of asymmetrical meter, with suggested groups marked

These asymmetrical meters are not as hard to perform as they might seem at first glance. The trick is to consider each measure as a combination of smaller regular beat groups. 5/4, for example, can be regarded as 2/4 + 3/4 or 3/4 + 2/4 (depending on the music — this is a matter of interpretation). 7/4 has more possibilities — it might seem to be written as 4/4 + 3/4, or 3/4 + 2/4 + 2/4, etc. Musicians often work out their interpretation of such meters bar by bar and then think of them that way while playing, as above.

Keeping notation simple

If you are writing down a rhythm to be played on an instrument whose sound stops quickly, such as a wood block or a snare drum, the use of rests is uncertain. For example, the following four patterns will all sound the same when played by an instrument whose tone does not sustain:

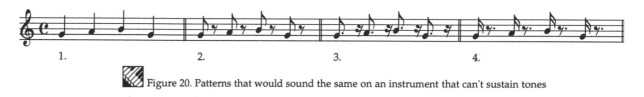

1.   2.   3.   4.

Figure 20. Patterns that would sound the same on an instrument that can't sustain tones

Musicians generally prefer to keep notation as simple as possible, and so a composer wanting short notes on a wood block would probably choose (2) or even (1) as the way to notate this pattern. Both performances would sound the same, and either one would be easier to write and read than (3) or (4). On the other hand, if the instrument were a violin each of these patterns would sound different, with long notes in (1) and very short notes in (4).

Notation does not tell you everything about how a passage will sound; you need to consider also what instrument is being used — as well as the tempo, the style of the piece, and other subtle factors.

Summary, Chapter II

1. Rhythmic notation is based on the concept of a steady underlying *beat*. Beats are grouped into *measures* of two, three, four, or more beats, the first of which is marked by a *metric accent*. Some meters also have a secondary accent on one of the other beats: 4/4 has a secondary accent on the third beat.

2. Measures are separated by *bar lines*, vertical lines through the staff. *Double bars* mark section divisions within the music; a heavy double bar marks the end of a piece. *Repeat bars* are different from other bar lines in that they don't necessarily mark the beginning or end of a measure; a repeat bar can occur within a measure.

3. The basic note value is the *whole note*, which can be divided into two *half notes* or four *quarter notes* or eight *eighth notes*, etc. The note values are distinguished by the symbol being filled-in or hollow, by the presence or absence of a *stem* and the presence or absence of one or more *flags*.

4. A *dot* after a note increases its value by one half, e.g., a dotted quarter note is as long as a quarter note plus an eighth note.

5. Flags may sometimes be replaced by *beams*, which are used to group notes in a way that makes the beat easier to see.

6. For every note value there is a corresponding *rest*, which indicates a length of silence.

7. A *meter signature* at the beginning of a score describes the metric organization of the music. Meters are either *simple*, in which the beat is counted with undotted notes or *compound*, in which the beat is counted with dotted notes.

8. In simple meter the upper number of the meter signature tells the number of beats counted per measure, while the lower number tells which note value corresponds to the beat. Examples: 2/2, 2/4, 4/8, 4/4, 3/4.

9. In a compound meter the upper number of the signature equals three times the number of beats actually counted in each bar. A fast 6/8 is generally performed compound, with 2 beats to the measure and each beat the value of a dotted quarter. Other examples of meter usually performed compound are 3/8, 9/8, and 12/8 (one, three, and four beats per bar).

10. A *duple* meter is one whose counted beats per measure can be divided by two. A triple meter divides by three. Examples of duple meter are 2/2, 2/4, 4/4, compound 6/8. Examples of *triple* meter are 3/4 and compound 9/8.

11. Stems may go either up or down without affecting the rhythm. Usually notes above the middle line of a staff have their stems downward; notes on or below the middle line have their stems upward.

12. *Asymmetrical* meters are those that divide neither by two nor three, such as 5/4 and 7/8. It is best to think of these as a combination of duple and triple meters — for instance, 5/4 can be read as 2/4 + 3/4 or 3/4 + 2/4, depending on the rhythmic groups within each measure.

III. READING RHYTHM

Vocalizing the Beat

There are several ways to go about reading an unfamiliar rhythm. One of them is to vocalize the beat aloud or in your head: count each beat and *subdivide* to match the smallest note values appearing in the passage. Figure 1 demonstrates counting with the beat subdivided in halves:

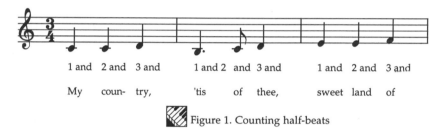

Figure 1. Counting half-beats

If there are sixteenth notes in the music you can add two more syllables and count the beat divided in fours, again speaking each syllable at a steady rate, like the ticking of a clock. For example:

Figure 2. Counting quarter-beats

Since each beat of a compound meter divides in three parts you could count a 6/8 measure with "One-and-a, Two-and-a," like this:

Figure 3. Counting in compound meter

The basic principle of rhythmic vocalizing is to speak steadily at the speed of the shortest note in the passage, and to use numbers to identify each beat. The actual syllables you speak don't matter, of course: for beats divided in two or three you could just as easily say "One wump Two wump" and "One bop bop Two bop bop." All that matters is that the counts are evenly spaced. Nor do you have to count out loud: the counting can all be in your head.

1 and 2 and   3 and   1 and 2   and 3   and

 Figure 4. Working out counting for a typical melody

Figure 4 shows how you would work out the counting for a typical melody. In this 3/4 example there are three beats to a bar, each equal to a quarter note, and the shortest note is an eighth. An eighth note is therefore one-half a beat, so we'll divide each beat into two equally-spaced syllables. A half note is worth four eighth notes, so it will receive four syllables.

Mental Conducting

Another help in reading rhythm is to "conduct" the music in your imagination. In fact, even when you already understand the rhythm, mental conducting is a good way to keep your place without losing the beat. Before trying mental conducting you should practice some actual conducting movements, as follows.

Try swinging your arm loosely from side to side, noticing how it accelerates into the bottom of the swing and slows down as it approaches the top of each swing, just like a pendulum. Once your arm is swinging in a relaxed and free manner, slowly bring your wrist up by bending your elbow and reduce the movement until only your forearm is swinging back and forth from left to right — with a downward emphasis on the outward swing. Now you are beating the time in two, as in 2/2 or 2/4, or 6/8 (remember that 6/8 usually has two beats per measure).

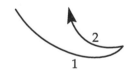

Figure 5. Conducting in two

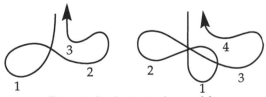

Figure 6. Conducting in three and four

You can use a similar motion of the arm to swing into these other patterns, which indicate 3 and 4 beats per measure (the illustrations are for the right arm — everything is reversed if you are lefthanded). The numbers in the drawings are placed roughly at the "bottom" of the swings to show you that there's a slight downward emphasis marking each beat. Remember also that the drawings are only approximate!

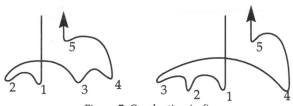

Figure 7. Conducting in five

To conduct an asymmetrical meter you need to think about how the rhythm is divided within each measure. For example, 5/4 can be either 2 + 3 or 3 + 2. As in the other diagrams, these illustrations are only approximate! Few conductors will follow such a pattern precisely.

 Open the Textbook Activity *3.1. Begin Reading Rhythms*. This activity will give you practice in reading various examples of rhythmic notation. All you have to do is to tap the middle row of computer keys in the rhythm of the notes on the screen, keeping in careful time with the beat as marked by the metronome (the metronome will subdivide the beat for you if you choose that option in the Tempo window). Don't worry about pitches! They will be supplied automatically for this activity.

Like any musical instrument, the computer keys have a preferred technique for a good performance. Alternate two fingers of one hand to play two keys of that middle row (the row that starts with A) and keep your fingers close to the keys as you play. Don't strike hard; a light touch works better. This is a fun way to practice reading rhythm notation, and hearing the pitches as you tap adds to the interest.

More on Metric Accents

In chapter 2 we mentioned that different meters can be recognized by their metric accents. Each measure begins with a strong *primary accent* on its first beat and certain meters can also have a weaker *secondary accent*, such as the secondary accent on the third beat in 4/4.

The metric accents are a natural consequence of repeated patterns. Suppose, for example, that you try saying the numbers "one two three four" out loud for a while, keeping a steady rhythm as if you were counting beats. Your counting will probably start to sound like this, sooner or later:

$$1\ {}_2\ 3\ {}_4\ 1\ {}_2\ 3\ {}_4\ 1\ {}_2\ 3\ {}_4$$

The largest numerals represent the primary accent, the midsize numerals the *secondary accent*, and the smallest ones (2 and 4 in 4/4 time) mark the *weak beats*.

Depending on your listening habits, you might also find yourself falling into the reverse of the above. Rock music often tends to emphasize the weak beats:

₁ **2** ₃ **4** ₁ **2** ₃ **4** !!

This off-center emphasis of rock does not actually change the strong nature of the first and third beats, however. It's really a kind of *syncopation* (see the next chapter), which gives a special emphasis to weak beats with the understanding that they will still be perceived as weak. Pop musicians sometimes refer to these "misplaced" accents as *backbeat*. So the melody is designed to have its important notes on the strong beats, while the accompaniment emphasizes the two and four, as in the stereotypical rock tune at right:

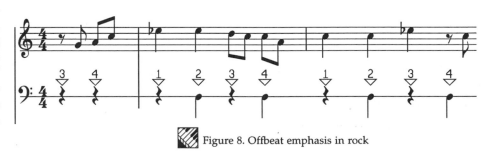

Figure 8. Offbeat emphasis in rock

No matter what sort of music you listen to, it will be difficult to avoid falling into the following pattern when counting three-beat measures:

1 ₂ ₃ **1** ₂ ₃ **1** ₂ ₃ **1** ₂ ₃

In a triple meter like this one both the second and third beats are weak.

If you compare these emphasis patterns to the conducting patterns you'll see that conducting expresses visually the same metric accents. This is most obvious in a simple two-beat, where the outward and downward swing of the hand has stronger character than the inward and upward swing — it represents the stronger *downbeat* while the return of the hand marks the weak *upbeat*.

In a four-beat conducting pattern there is a similar emphasis: the long motion from left to right tends to give the "three" almost as much weight as the "one," dividing the measure into two halves of two beats each. When conducting in 3/4, on the other hand, the measure doesn't seem to divide in any way except in three. In all the patterns the downbeat has what seems like the greatest importance, and the last beat of the measure is a preparation for the next downbeat.

Be careful not to overdo metric accents; they will come naturally without much deliberate effort to produce them. The accented note doesn't have to be louder than the others — it might only be held a little longer. Sometimes the accents are indicated well enough by the harmonic accompaniment (perhaps a new harmony will be played on the accented notes). In some cases proper expression can even require suppressing metric accents altogether. Generally, however, the metric accents should be communicated because they give each meter its character; they are part of the reason why a musician can hear that a piece is in 3/4 rather than 6/8 without seeing the music.

As an example of the effect of meter on a melodic pattern let's look at the metric accents in two different versions of the same melody, the same melody that was used in chapter 2 to illustrate the need for careful use of beams. This tune would be conducted in three beats if written in 3/4, and its accents would fall on the first note of each pair, especially the first note of the measure, which carries the primary accent.

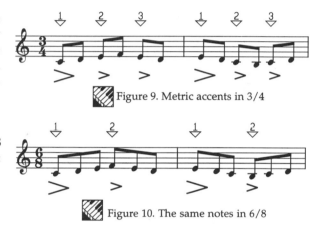

Figure 9. Metric accents in 3/4

The choice of "important notes" would come out differently in a 6/8 version of the same pattern, which would be conducted in two instead of three:

Figure 10. The same notes in 6/8

The computer, unfortunately, plays these examples both the same, since it doesn't have the flexibility to interpret metric accents properly—despite the fact that you can give some impression of metric accent by turning on the metronome. The machine could be programmed to make the accented notes always louder, but that would get tiresome. Making them always longer would also get old after a while. A human musician considers the desired expression, the speed of performance, the way the melody is moving, the nature of the accompaniment, the phrasing — and then adjusts in whatever way will make that particular piece most effective. The only way to learn that art is by listening to good performers. Which brings us to the topic of music that goes....

Beyond the Written Note

It's important to remember that the notation of rhythm, like all music notation, is not meant to be a complete mathematical description of the sound — a complete description would be very complicated and hard to read. Written music requires some additional interpretation. Great performers rarely play the same piece twice in the same way, yet all their performances are correct readings; what we are doing now is *just the first step* — learning to understand the basic design provided by the notation.

The additions made in interpretation are often subtle and may take experience to appreciate fully. In a group of quarter notes that all look the same on the page some may be played with more "air" between them, a variation that falls under the heading of change in *articulation*. And there may sometimes be a certain freedom with the time, which is known as *rubato* and which may include speeding up (*accelerando*) or slowing down (*ritardando*). A note may sometimes be brought into prominence by an *agogic accent* — an accent produced by playing the note a tiny bit early or late (the word *agogic* refers to all accents made by changes in note length or timing). And here we're only speaking of rhythmic variation; there are many other ways that two performances can vary without either being incorrect.

An easy-to-hear example of rhythmic freedom is found in most performances of the beginning of the *Blue Danube* waltz by Johann Strauss. The *rubato* described below does not appear in the score but almost everyone plays it that way, and it works very well:

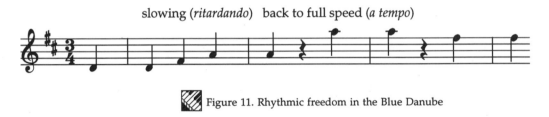

 Figure 11. Rhythmic freedom in the Blue Danube

That graceful slowing to a slight pause, followed by a return to the normal tempo, gives an effect that might be compared to coasting over the top of a hill on a bicycle: just briefly one reaches a point of stillness, and then movement starts again. It's perfect for an invitation to a dance, and this interpretation has become a tradition with Viennese waltz music.

Now that you've tried reading written rhythms you are prepared to attempt reversing the process and writing down rhythms that you hear. The Textbook Activity *3.2. Writing Rhythms* offers an introduction to what later will become melodic dictation — a valuable skill for anyone who wants to compose.

Summary, Chapter III

1. Counting a rhythm out loud or in your head is one way to learn an unfamiliar rhythm. It helps to *subdivide* each beat into halves, quarters, or thirds, as appropriate. Beats can be counted in halves using the syllable "and" for the half-beats: "One and Two and Three and Four and." You can further divide by adding more syllables: "One-e-and-a two-e-and-a three-e-and-a four-e-and-a" for beats divided in four parts. In a compound meter each beat can be divided in threes by saying, "One and a Two and a, etc."

2. The conducting patterns will also guide you in understanding rhythm. They help you to keep your place and also indicate the metric accents of each meter.

3. Music in 4/4 time has a primary accent on the first beat and a secondary accent on the third beat, while 3/4 accents just the first beat. 6/8 meter is conducted in two, like 2/4, so it has its primary accent on the first beat; it may also have a secondary accent at the beginning of the second beat if the melody is moving in eighth notes. These metric accents are shown sometimes by greater loudness, sometimes by greater length of accented notes, sometimes by harmonic changes in the accompaniment. Sometimes the performed accents can contrast the accents of the meter, as in rock music's emphasis of offbeats.

4. Reading an asymmetrical meter is easier if you group its beats into threes and twos. These submetrical groupings are reflected in the conducting patterns for asymmetrical meters.

5. Written music requires interpretation — the printed music is not a literal transcription. An understanding of performance traditions is needed to perform written music well.

IV. COMPLEX RHYTHM

The Tie

The *tie* joins two notes of the same pitch so that they sound like one. Sometimes you can use a tie to mean the same thing as a dot:

The tie can also be used to make notes of a length that can't be created with dots, such as a quarter note plus a sixteenth. And a tie is the only way to hold a note over a bar line:

Another important purpose of the tie is to make the beat groupings clear within a measure:

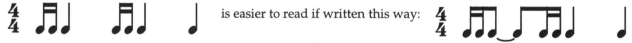

is easier to read if written this way:

Figures 1-4. Use of the tie

Syncopation

Syncopation is something you probably know well without being aware of it. It gives vivacity to rhythm and is an important part of jazz and popular music, as well as being a frequent device in the classics. To syncopate you just begin a note on an "offbeat" (anywhere other than the beginning of a beat) and carry it over to the next beat. It creates an effect that might be described as "starting the note early."

Figure 5. Syncopation is marked with *

Usually the word "syncopation" refers to notes that are held over as above. But in a more general sense any rhythm that emphasizes the offbeats could be called "syncopated":

Figure 6. Syncopation by accents in Stravinsky's *Sacre du printemps*

When syncopated notes are held over to the next beat the beat groups will be easier to see if you use ties. But simple patterns such as syncopated quarter notes are so common that they are often written without ties, as in the beginning of Haydn's Symphony No.45:

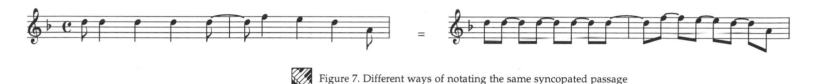

Figure 7. Different ways of notating the same syncopated passage

 Launch the Textbook Activity *4.1. Reading Syncopation*. This activity is similar to earlier activities in reading rhythm, but the examples will include more complex rhythms that involve syncopation.

Hemiola

Hemiola is a special kind of syncopation. You could use this term for any syncopation that causes the effect of duple meter within the context of triple meter, or vice-versa. In both of the following examples the second measure uses hemiola: in the first case three quarter notes are played in the time of two beats (remember that 6/8 has two beats to the bar); in the second example two dotted quarters are played in the time of three beats.

Figure 8. Two examples of *hemiola*

Triplets, Duplets, and Tuplets

We've seen that all undotted notes divide only in twos, fours, eights, etc. What if you want to fit three equal notes into the time of a single undotted quarter note?

You can do it by marking each group with the number "3," as follows:

The grouping is called a *triplet*, and it is especially effective when used as Mozart uses it here, in contrast to duple rhythm. The "3" means that three notes are to be played in the time of two. In the Mozart, three triplet eighth notes are played in the time of two normal eighth notes, i.e., in the time of a quarter note. The below illustration shows how you would notate triplets having the time value of a half note, a quarter note, or an eighth note:

Figure 9. Triplets in Mozart's Piano Concerto, K. 467

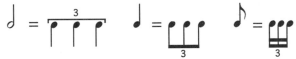

Contrasting the triplet is the *duplet*, an occasion where you play only two equal notes in the time of what would be three:

    Figure 10. A duplet

That duplet rhythm could be notated literally, using dotted notes:  Figure 11. A duplet notated with dotted notes

You could also write five eighth notes to fit in the time of four normal eighth notes, and mark this *quintuplet* with a "5":

Figure 12. A quintuplet

The word *tuplet* can be used as a general term for all irregular groups other than the triplet. The performance of large tuplets can sometimes be flexible. Here's a very large irregular grouping by Chopin, a group of nineteen sixteenth notes played in the time of twelve:

Naturally Chopin didn't really expect the musician to play nineteen notes in mathematically exact time! What he intended was that the pianist should use a free, improvisatory style for these notes. But smaller groups like triplets really must be precise for a good effect.

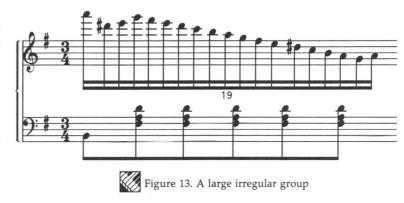

Figure 13. A large irregular group

From the Textbook Activities folder please choose *4.2. Reading Triplets*. Reading these is not as hard as you might think; try listening to each example before you press the "Begin" button. Once you are accomplished at reading triplets alone you can try Level 4 of 2-part Rhythm Reading (in the Activities folder) for the more difficult challenge of playing duple with one hand and triple with the other.

Summary, Chapter IV

1. A *tie* joins two notes so that they sound like one. Ties can be used to hold notes over a bar line, to make notes of a length that can't be made with dots, such as a quarter plus a sixteenth, and also to visually clarify the beat groups in a measure.

2. *Syncopated* notes are those that begin offbeat and avoid any accent on the downbeat.

3. *Hemiola* is a type of syncopation that creates the effect of duple meter within the context of triple meter, or vice-versa.

4. A *triplet* is a group of three notes played in the time allotted for two. It is marked with a "3." Similarly, a *duplet* is a group of two notes that sounds in the time that would normally be taken by three. *Tuplet* is a general term for other irregular groupings, such as the *quintuplet*.

V. INTERVALS

Naming Intervals

The difference in pitch between two notes is referred to as an *interval*. If the two notes are played at the same time the interval is a *harmonic interval*, and if they are played one after the other the proper term is *melodic interval*.

The intervals are named according to the number of scale notes they include. That's equivalent to saying that they are named for the number of staff lines and spaces they include, or the number of letter names. For instance, the interval from C to G covers five lines and spaces or five letters, counting its starting and ending notes: C (D, E, F,) G, so it is called a *fifth*. Similarly, D to F is a *third*: D, (E), F. D to F♯ is also a third, but a different kind. E to F covers only two letters, so it's a *second*. C to C♯ is a type of *unison*, since it includes only one letter, and so is C to C or C to Cb. Figure 1 shows the basic intervals in harmonic form.

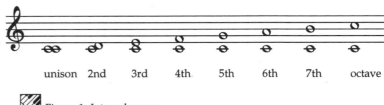

unison 2nd 3rd 4th 5th 6th 7th octave

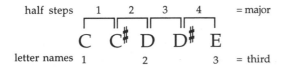 Figure 1. Interval names

Major and Minor Intervals

Each type of interval can have different *qualities*, which are determined by counting half steps. The quality of seconds, thirds, sixths, and sevenths can be *major* or *minor*. A *major third* such as C-E, includes four half steps and is a half step larger than a *minor third* like D-F, which has only three half steps.

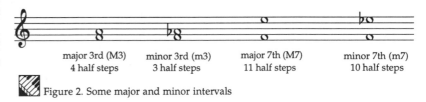

| major 3rd (M3) | minor 3rd (m3) | major 7th (M7) | minor 7th (m7) |
| 4 half steps | 3 half steps | 11 half steps | 10 half steps |

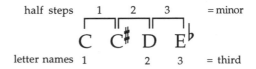 Figure 2. Some major and minor intervals

Be careful: when counting half steps we are not counting the notes but rather the spaces between them:

half steps 1 2 3 4 = major

C C♯ D D♯ E

letter names 1   2   3 = third

half steps 1 2 3 = minor

C C♯ D E♭

letter names 1   2   3 = third

Perfect intervals

Unisons, *fifths*, *fourths*, and *octaves* cannot be called major or minor; they have one basic quality, which is *perfect*. A *perfect fifth*, for example, has seven half steps; a *perfect fourth* has five half steps.

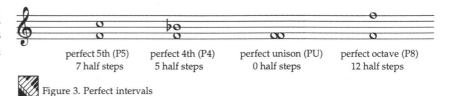

| perfect 5th (P5) | perfect 4th (P4) | perfect unison (PU) | perfect octave (P8) |
| 7 half steps | 5 half steps | 0 half steps | 12 half steps |

 Figure 3. Perfect intervals

Augmented and Diminished Intervals

If a major or perfect interval is enlarged by one half step it is an *augmented* interval. If a minor or perfect interval is reduced one half step it is *diminished*. For example, F to A♯ is a third (it includes three letter names) but it has five half steps, one half step larger than major, so it is an augmented third. B to F (going upward) is spelled as a fifth, B (C, D, E,) F, but it has only six half steps, so it is a *diminished fifth*. D rising to F♭ is a third that is one half step smaller than minor, so it is a diminished third. Augmented and diminished intervals are identified with the signs "+ " and "°."

| perfect 5th (P5) | augmented 5th (+5) | diminished 5th (°5) | major 3rd (M3) | minor 3rd (m3) | augmented 3rd (+3) | diminished 3rd (°3) |
| 7 half steps | 8 half steps | 6 half steps | 4 half steps | 3 half steps | 5 half steps | 2 half steps |

Figure 4. Augmenting and diminishing the perfect and major/minor intervals

Interval Chart

To identify an interval correctly you must do two things: first get the numeric name of the interval by counting the number of letter names it covers, and then count the half steps in it to determine its quality. This chart of the most common intervals will help. Notice that two possible answers are given for each size in half steps. An augmented second and a minor third, for example, both have three half steps.

half steps	0	1	2	3	4	5	6	7	8	9	10	11	12
name	P1 or °2	m2 or +1	M2 or °3	m3 or +2	M3 or °4	P4 or +3	+4 or °5	P5 or °6	m6 or +5	M6 or °7	m7 or +6	M7 or °8	P8 or +7

Beyond Augmented and Diminished

In theory, intervals can even be *doubly* or *triply* augmented or diminished but you won't often see such oddities. If you did encounter an interval such as A♭ rising to D♯, however, you could analyze it this way: it includes four letter names (A,B,C,D), so it's a fourth, and it has seven half steps, which is one greater than an augmented fourth. Therefore it's a *doubly-augmented fourth*.

 Launch the Textbook Activity *5.1. Identifying Intervals.* This activity will display intervals and ask you to identify them by clicking on one of several choices. It will do something else, too — if you play two notes on the keyboard it will tell you what interval they form. This offers a way to get the answer to each question, and it can also be used if you are curious about the name of a particular interval.

Identifying Intervals Quickly

One aid to interval identification is to memorize the qualities of the "natural intervals," which are the intervals as they appear in the C major scale, with no sharps or flats. Then you can use them as standards with which to compare intervals that do have sharps or flats.

For example, all natural fifths or fourths on the staff are perfect except those between B and F. So if you see a non-natural fifth like C-G♯ you remember that the natural fifth C-G is perfect, and since this one's upper note is raised a half step it must be one half step larger than perfect.   So C-G♯ is an augmented fifth. Similarly, all natural thirds are either major or minor.

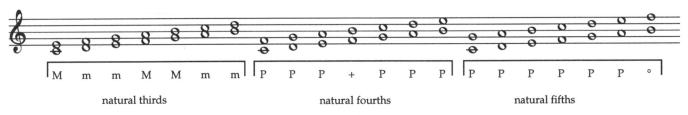

natural thirds   natural fourths   natural fifths

 Figure 5. The natural thirds and fifths

It is very important to memorize the qualities of the natural thirds and fifths . When you see B ascending to D you will know instantly that B-D is a minor third, containing 3 half steps. So if you encounter instead a B♭-D you'll know that since the B is now lowered a half step the interval has gotten larger than its natural version and therefore it must be a major third.

Even simpler is the case of an interval that is just like a natural one except that both of its notes have been raised or lowered by the same amount. This, of course, has no effect on the name of the interval, which remains the same in both numeric size and quality:

P5   P5   P5

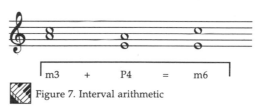

Figure 6. Identical modifiers leave the quality unchanged.

Knowing the qualities of the natural thirds and the natural fifths/fourths will also help you to quickly determine the qualities of other intervals. For example, a sixth can be regarded as a perfect fourth added to a third (note that this isn't quite like arithmetic — in musical intervals 4 + 3 equals 6!). *Adding a perfect interval never changes the quality of the result*, so if the sixth looks like a minor third plus a perfect fourth then the sixth itself must be minor, too (figure 7).

m3   +   P4   =   m6

Figure 7. Interval arithmetic

Similarly, a seventh could be seen as a third added to a perfect fifth. So a major third on top of a perfect fifth must add up to a major seventh (figure 8).

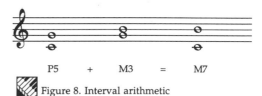

P5   +   M3   =   M7

Figure 8. Interval arithmetic

Inverting Intervals

If you reverse the notes of an interval you obtain its *inversion*. For example, C rising to E is a major third; its inversion is E rising to C, a minor sixth. Knowing the principle of inversion is handy for quick recognition, because *inversion reverses an interval's quality*. Major intervals become minor upon inversion; diminished intervals become augmented. Perfect intervals, however, remain perfect. As for the number of the interval, it is always 9 minus the old number: a sixth, for example, will invert to a third (9 minus 6 equals 3).

So if you see the note C with a B above it, you can use the inversion principle to quickly identify the interval as a major seventh: if the B were below the C it would be a minor second away (that's easier to count out than a seventh), and a minor second inverts to a major seventh (minor inverts to major; 9 minus 2 equals 7).

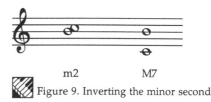

m2   M7

Figure 9. Inverting the minor second

Launch the Textbook Activity *5.2. Speed Intervals* and see if you can score the required points. Speed counts in this activity, so your command of the material will be tested more thoroughly.

More about Enharmonic Equivalents

You can easily make a mistake in identifying or writing intervals if you don't distinguish between notes that are *enharmonic equivalents* such as F♯ and G♭ or E and F♭ (*enharmonic equivalents* are notes or intervals or chords that are spelled differently and yet use the same keys on a piano).

A second, the difference between any two adjacent scale steps, will always be spelled with two adjacent letter names. F to G♭ is a second, as are F to G and F to G♯. However, F to F♯ is not a second but a kind of unison, since it involves only one letter name — even though the F♯ is played on the same piano key as the G♭.

What matters for naming an interval is not how it sounds, but how it is written on the staff.

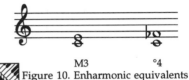

Similarly, a third such as C to E is not at all the same thing as C to F♭, though the two use the same piano keys and have the same number of half steps. C to F♭ would actually be called a kind of fourth — in this case a diminished fourth — because it includes four letter names: C, D, E, F, and yet has one half step less than an ordinary perfect fourth like C-F.

Figure 10. Enharmonic equivalents

This distinction is not just a matter of being fussy about technicalities. The choice of name for a note can provide information about that note's role in the music: in some circumstances, for example, D♯ could imply that a note is on its way upward to E, while E♭ might mean that the direction is downward to D. Most importantly, the use of the correct name has important implications for understanding *harmony,* which will be the subject of later chapters, and it can even affect the actual performed pitch, if the instrument is one with freely variable pitch. For example, depending on the musical context, a violinist presented with a sharp accidental may tend to play the modified note higher in pitch than its equivalent flat.

Compound Intervals

If you add an octave to an interval its quality is unchanged. Such intervals are known as *compound intervals:*

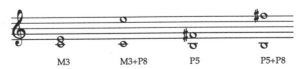

Figure 11. Compound intervals

Sometimes specific names are used for these: a second plus an octave is a *ninth,* a third plus an octave is a *tenth,* a fourth plus an octave is an *eleventh,* then come the *twelfth* and the *thirteenth.* But there it stops; you will not hear of fourteenths or fifteenths.

Consonant and Dissonant Intervals

One of the most misunderstood concepts in all of music is that of *dissonance*. Dissonance is the name given to the quality of "disagreement" or "instability" that we may perceive between two or more simultaneous notes; it contrasts the feeling of *consonance* that we notice in other cases. We say, for example, that a second is dissonant, but a fifth is consonant, as in figure 12:

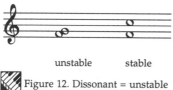

unstable   stable

Figure 12. Dissonant = unstable

All that is meant by this distinction is that the dissonant interval is less stable; it gives the impression that it is ready to move. You will sometimes hear dissonance defined as an "unpleasant" quality, but most musicians would argue that, on the contrary, dissonance is quite enjoyable. Dissonance has always been the delight of composers, whose work would be static and empty without it, and many of our favorite moments in music depend on a dissonant effect. But, in *tonal music of the style we are studying* — that is, music based on major and minor scales and using chords in the manner we'll discuss later — it is essential that dissonances be treated carefully: usually their best effect will require that they be followed quickly by a contrasting consonant interval as part of what is called *resolution* of the dissonance. For now let's just determine which intervals are considered consonant and which are dissonant.

The stable or consonant intervals are the unison, the octave, the fifth, third, and sixth:

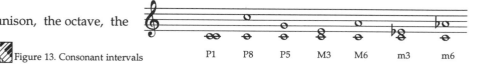

Figure 13. Consonant intervals

P1   P8   P5   M3   M6   m3   m6

All other intervals are unstable or dissonant: the second, seventh, and every augmented or diminished interval, especially the augmented fourth and diminished fifth:

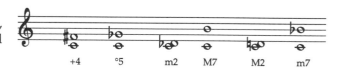

Figure 14. Dissonant intervals

+4   °5   m2   M7   M2   m7

The perfect fourth is special: it's treated as dissonant only if one of its notes is the bass, or lowest note sounding. If it appears in the upper voices as part of a chord, then it's consonant.

Figure 15. Consonance of the fourth is variable

dissonant   consonant

When we reach the topic of voice-leading you'll see how dissonance is used to give movement and drama to music.

Please open the Textbook Activity *5.3. Building Intervals*. Practice building all of the common intervals beginning on any pitch, both ascending and descending, and Practica Musica will show you the correct answer if you make a mistake.

Enharmonic Dissonances

You may have noticed that certain dissonances are identical in sound, at least on a piano, with some of the consonances. For example, the augmented second and minor third sound the same on a piano; they are *enharmonic*, yet one is classed as dissonant while the other is consonant. Just remember that their "dissonance" is partly a matter of what they traditionally imply harmonically, and also that on some instruments the two can in fact sound different. In tonal music a dissonant spelling can indicate that the interval in question is not stable but rather is unsettled and about to change; the dissonant note could then be called a *tendency tone* that implies movement. To the eyes of a musician, the second note of a melodic augmented second is probably moving upward and may benefit from some stretching in that direction if it is being played on an instrument that allows flexibility of pitch. On the other hand, its enharmonic equivalent, the minor third, is more stable and has no such tendency. The significance of correctly-spelled dissonances will become more apparent when we reach the topic of chords.

Summary, Chapter V

1. Two notes of different pitch form an *interval*. If the notes are played at the same time we call it a *harmonic interval*; otherwise it's a *melodic interval*.

2. Intervals are named according to the number of letter names they include. C to G, C to G♯, and C to G♭, for instance, cover five letters, C, D, E, F, G, so they are all *fifths* of some kind. Other intervals are the *unison, second, third, fourth, sixth, seventh, and octave.*

3. The second, third, sixth, and seventh have two basic qualities, called *major* and *minor*. The minor form of each interval is a half step smaller than the major form. C-E is a *major third*; C-E♭ is a *minor third*.

4. The unison, octave, fifth and fourth have one basic quality, called *perfect*. C-G is a *perfect fifth*.

5. If an interval is a half step larger than major or perfect, it is *augmented*. If it is a half step smaller than minor or perfect, it is *diminished*. C-E♭♭ is a *diminished third* and C-E♯ is an *augmented third*. C-G♯ is an *augmented fifth*; C-G♭ is a *diminished fifth*.

6. If the order of notes in an interval is reversed, you obtain its *inversion*. The number of an inverted interval is always 9 minus the number of the uninverted interval, and the *quality* (major-minor, diminished-augmented) of an interval reverses when it is inverted. Example: the M3 C-E inverts to the m6 E-C. However, the quality of a perfect interval remains perfect when inverted.

7. Intervals that use the same keys on the piano but are spelled differently, such as the augmented third C-E♯ and the perfect fourth C-F, are known as *enharmonic equivalents*. They have different musical meanings and functions despite being the same on the piano.

8. A *compound interval* is one that has been increased by one or more octaves. Some compound intervals have interval names: a *ninth* is the same as a second plus an octave, a *tenth* is the same as a third plus an octave; other names for large intervals are the *eleventh* (fourth plus octave), *twelfth* (fifth plus octave), and *thirteenth* (sixth plus octave).

9. *Consonance* refers to the feeling of stability produced by certain intervals such as the unison, octave, fifth, third, and sixth. *Dissonance* is the instability associated with intervals such as the second, seventh, augmented fourth or diminished fifth. In tonal music the perfect fourth is considered dissonant when one of its notes is the bass, or current lowest note in the harmony.

VI. SCALES AND KEY SIGNATURES

Scale Degrees

Each of the seven notes of a major or minor scale has a name. These names will be convenient when describing scales and later will be used in harmony, too, so this is a good moment to learn them.

The first note of any scale is the *tonic*. Next in ascending order come the *supertonic, mediant, subdominant, dominant, submediant,* and *subtonic.* The logic behind these names is clear if you view a scale with its tonic in the center:

tonic

subtonic   supertonic

submediant   mediant

subdominant   dominant

Figure 1. Scale degrees

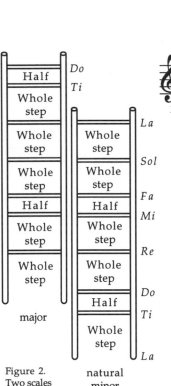

Figure 2.
Two scales

major   natural
minor

The three most important notes of the scale are the tonic, the dominant, and the subdominant, which for historical and acoustical reasons form something like foundation posts for the scale: the dominant is a fifth above the tonic; the subdominant a fifth below. The mediant, the third degree of the scale, gets its name from being halfway between the tonic and the dominant; in a sense it mediates between them. The submediant mediates between the tonic and the subdominant. Finally there's the supertonic, just above the tonic, and the subtonic, just below it. When the subtonic is only a half step from the tonic, as in a major scale, it can also be called the *leading tone* because it seems to lead back to the tonic.

The Natural Minor Scale

The major scale discussed in chapter 2 has a close relation in the *natural minor*. The same white key pattern used for the major scale produces the natural minor if you begin with A instead of C. Put another way, you can sing a natural minor scale with the familiar solmization syllables by beginning with La instead of Do: *La, Ti, Do, Re, Mi, Fa, Sol.* The natural minor scale can be expressed as the following pattern of whole and half steps: W H W W H W W, as in the ladder at left.

Relative Minor and Relative Major

Because the minor scale beginning on A uses the same notes as the major scale on C, we say that the a minor scale is the *relative minor* of C major, and C major is the *relative major* of the a minor scale. In the C major scale A is *La*, the sixth or submediant degree, and similarly, every major scale, no matter what note it starts on, has a relative minor scale that begins with its submediant and which shares the same set of pitches and uses the same sharps or flats. Since the submediant is either a major sixth above or a minor third below the tonic, you can also find the relative minor by counting down a minor third from the tonic note of a major scale. For example, to find the relative minor of a major scale beginning on F♯, you need to count downward from F♯ to D♯: d♯ minor is the relative minor of F♯ major. Conversely, you can find the relative major of a minor scale by counting up a minor third from the tonic.

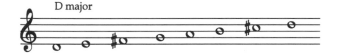

 Figure 3. Major scale and its relative natural minor

Parallel Minor and Parallel Major

The *parallel minor* of a major scale is the minor scale with the same tonic, and necessarily must use some notes that are not part of its parallel major. Again the example shows the "natural" form of the minor scale, which you can see uses several flats in this case. The natural minor is not necessarily made of naturals; it is called that because it uses only the unaltered tones of its relative major scale.

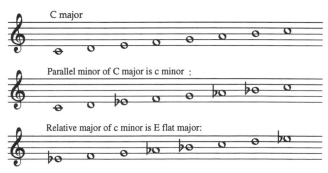

 Figure 4. Parallel minor vs. relative minor

Key Signatures

When writing the notes of the E flat major and c minor scales for figure 4 it was necessary to include several flats. E flat major and c minor don't use E♮; they use E♭, and also the flat forms of B and A. Rather than write the flats every time those notes appear, it is customary to show them at the left of the page in a *key signature*. The key signature of three flats tells the reader that any B, E, or A in the music is to be played as a flat unless otherwise indicated. To a musician that signature would identify the piece as one that uses either the E flat major scale or the c minor scale: the piece would have to be either in the *key of E flat*, or the *key of c minor*. The choice would depend on the nature of the music and its harmony.

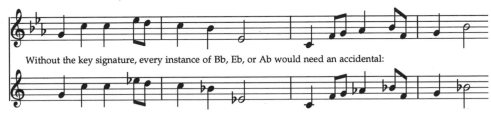

Without the key signature, every instance of Bb, Eb, or Ab would need an accidental:

Figure 5. A melody with and without a key signature

A key signature is printed at the beginning of each line and stays in effect until canceled by another one. Whenever you write a clef you should follow it by the key signature.

Traditional key signatures are composed either of flats or sharps, not both, and the flats and sharps are always added in the same order: the first flat is always B♭ and the first sharp is always F♯. Subsequent flats are each a fifth lower than the previous one and subsequent sharps are each a fifth higher than the previous one. This helps you to quickly identify the notes—if a key has only two sharps in its signature they will always be F♯ and C♯: you don't need to look at their placement in the staff.

The flats or sharps are displayed in a standard arrangement to make them easier to recognize. Here are all fifteen signatures and their keys, as drawn in the treble and bass clefs. Major keys are listed in upper case, minor in lower.

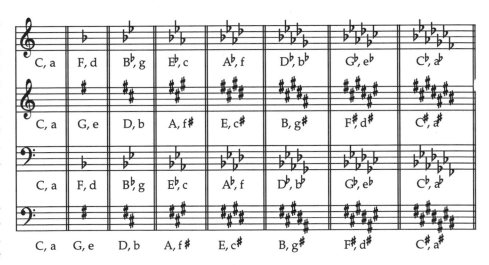

Figure 6. Table of key signatures

The Circle of Fifths

Starting with C, whenever a tonic rises a fifth, another sharp is added to the key signature. Going in the other direction from C, when the tonic drops a fifth another flat is added to the signature. This simple but elegant principle is traditionally represented by the *circle of fifths*. The circular design helps to show how the two series begin to overlap with their enharmonic equivalents after reaching five sharps or flats, but the same information can as easily be represented by the straight chart below. In both these charts lower-case letters are used to refer to the minor keys:

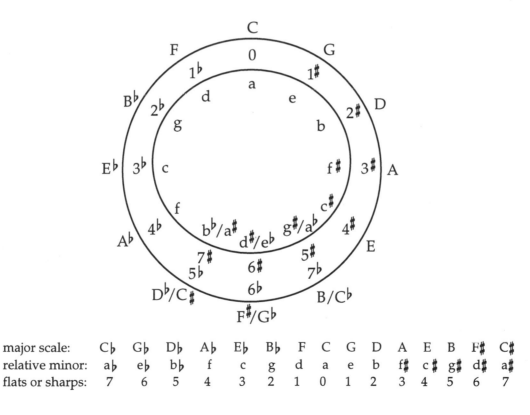

major scale:	C♭	G♭	D♭	A♭	E♭	B♭	F	C	G	D	A	E	B	F♯	C♯
relative minor:	a♭	e♭	b♭	f	c	g	d	a	e	b	f♯	c♯	g♯	d♯	a♯
flats or sharps:	7	6	5	4	3	2	1	0	1	2	3	4	5	6	7

Figure 7. Circle of fifths

Identifying Keys From the Signature

Usually students just memorize the signatures: one sharp means G major or e minor; two means D major or b minor, etc. But there is a shortcut to identifying a key from its signature. Notice that the last sharp in a key signature is always the seventh degree of the major scale for that key.

The last sharp in this signature is D♯, which must then be the seventh degree of the major key using this signature, so the major key tonic is the next note up, E. This signature must be for E major or its relative minor, c♯ minor.

In flat signatures, the last flat is the fourth degree of the corresponding major scale.

Here the last flat is D♭, so the major scale using this signature is four scale steps downward: A♭. The piece must be either in A♭ major or its relative minor, f (or: if there's more than one flat, the next-to-last is the tonic).

Of course, both of these methods require that you know whether the piece is major or minor! For now you can generally just check the last note of the piece, which is almost always the tonic: a piece with a two-sharp key signature that ends on B is probably in b minor rather than D major. Once you learn chords there will be no doubt of the key, but that comes later.

Accidentals in the Context of a Key

If you see an accidental — a written sharp, flat, natural, double-sharp, or double-flat not in the key signature — it means that the changed note is not part of the prevailing major scale or natural minor scale, since the key signature supplies all the scale notes for major and natural minor. Accidentals apply only to the note they precede — not to other octaves of the same pitch class — and they last until the end of the measure. If the altered note is used again in the next measure then a new accidental must be written.

Figure 10. Accidentals in context

In the last measure of figure 10 the second B♭ doesn't need an accidental. The flat is still in effect from earlier in the measure.

Precautionary Accidentals

Since accidentals last only until the next measure line, you have to write them again if you want to repeat the same accidental in the next measure. Nonetheless, composers often remind the reader that an accidental is no longer in effect by marking the note explicitly with a *precautionary accidental* in the next measure, like this:

Figure 11. A precautionary accidental

accidental   precautionary accidental

In this example the A would have reverted to A♭ anyway, but the flat was written in as a reminder.

 Launch the Textbook Activity *6.1. Reading in Keys* and practice reading pitches in the context of key signatures. The first part of this activity presents melodies that use key signatures but no accidentals; in the second part you will read accidentals in the context of key signatures.

The Harmonic Minor Scale

One of the most common reasons for using an accidental in a melody is to make use of an alternate form of the minor scale. The natural minor, as we have seen, uses only the notes designated by the key signature, but there are other minor scales. For example, composers often want to raise the seventh note of a minor scale to make it lead back to the tonic — in other words, they want to give it a *leading tone* such as the major scale has: a seventh note that is only one half step away from the tonic. To accomplish this, the seventh degree of the natural minor must be raised with an accidental of some sort, forming what we call the *harmonic minor* (when we get to chords you'll see why it's called that). For example:

Figure 12. Natural and harmonic minors

The harmonic form of the minor requires no changes in the key signature. The seventh degree is always raised by writing a sharp or natural as an accidental. Note also that when we alter a scale tone we *never change its letter name*. F becomes F♯, not G♭.

The Melodic Minor

Figure 13. Mystery interval

Now that you can identify intervals you'll be able to see that the harmonic minor scale has an unusual feature. What would you call the interval between its sixth and seventh degrees (figure 13) ?

This interval, the augmented second, was long regarded as awkward or at least exotic. When composers wanted to avoid the augmented second but still intended to use the raised seventh degree they raised the sixth degree as well, making the interval between the two an ordinary major second. Because the goal of this alteration was to produce smoother melody we call this form of minor the *melodic minor*:

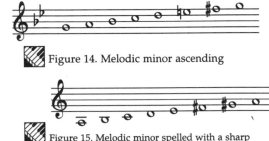

Figure 14. Melodic minor ascending

Notice that we raised the sixth degree by using a natural sign on what would otherwise have been an E♭. In other scales it might be necessary to use a sharp to get the same result, as in the melodic a minor scale:

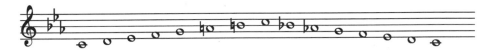

Figure 15. Melodic minor spelled with a sharp

You'll often see the melodic minor written in textbooks with two forms: one for going up and one for coming down:

Figure 16. Melodic minor ascending and descending

In practice there is usually no real need to define the melodic minor as having different forms for ascent and descent, because all three forms of the minor can be mixed in a single piece. The "descending melodic minor" is really just the natural minor again. On the other hand, the textbook definition of melodic minor gives us a handy way to describe tunes such as the Scottish folk song "Charlie Is My Darling," whose character depends on its use of both raised and natural sixth and seventh degrees that revert to their natural form when the movement is downward:

Figure 17. A traditional tune that uses melodic minor

'Twas   on a   Mon-day mor- ning, right   ear-ly   in the year,   when   Char- lie came to   our   town, the   young ca- va- li- er,...

The Pentatonic Scale

The pentatonic (five-tone) scale is found in folk music around the world as well as in composed music. Almost anything you play in the pentatonic scale sounds melodious because there's no way to make a dissonant leap: it contains no augmented fourth or diminished fifth. The typical major pentatonic scale is built in this pattern: whole step, whole step, minor third, whole step, minor third — just like the black keys of the piano, or like a major scale without the fourth and seventh degrees. If you play a melody using only black keys you are playing in a pentatonic scale.

"Amazing Grace" is a good example of a major pentatonic melody: its only pitches are F, G, A, C, and D.

 Figure 18. A major pentatonic melody

"Come All You Fair and Tender Maidens" is a different sort of pentatonic melody. Though it uses the same five notes as "Amazing Grace" it gives a minor effect by emphasizing the "D" and the minor third above it:

 Figure 19. A minor pentatonic melody

There are several possible forms of the pentatonic scale. Below are the major pentatonic, as found in "Amazing Grace", the minor, as found in "Come All You Fair and Tender Maidens," and an alternate form of the minor pentatonic.

major pentatonic   minor pentatonic   another minor pentatonic

 Figure 20. Several forms of the pentatonic scale

The Whole-tone Scale

As the name suggests, the whole-tone scale is composed entirely of whole steps. A non-traditional scale, it has no dominant, subdominant, or leading tone. Therefore you can't make any of its notes sound like a "tonic," which gives whole-tone music a sense of being adrift without a compass.

Figure 21. Whole tones from C

Claude Debussy often used the whole-tone scale:

Figure 22. Whole tones in Debussy's *Prélude à l'après-midi d'un faune*

The Octatonic Scale

This non-traditional eight-tone scale is associated with the work of Igor Stravinsky. It consists of alternating whole and half steps, and produces an effect that recalls a traditional minor, except that it lacks the tonic-dominant relationship.

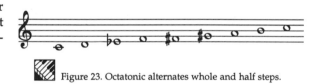

Figure 23. Octatonic alternates whole and half steps.

The Blues Scale

Blues musicians sing and play in a scale that is like a major scale but with ambiguous third, seventh, and sometimes sixth degrees. The variable degrees tend to be more often minor than major, but what really distinguishes blues music is the fact that the harmony is always derived from the major scale, and the often-lowered variable degrees in the

Figure 24. The blues scale

melody clash with the harmony. This makes the blues scale somewhat different from the major and minor scales, in which the harmony is formed from the scale degrees. The blues scale is therefore hard to represent in a way that communicates its real character, but this is close.

The Church Modes

The major and minor scales are the survivors of a number of scales or *modes* that date from medieval times. The modes are still occasionally heard today, especially in folk music and jazz. You can get something of an idea of the flavor of the modes if you play just the white keys using D, E, F, or G as a tonic. The mode starting on D is known as the *Dorian* mode; E is the tonic for the *Phrygian*; F for the *Lydian*, and G for the *MixoLydian*. The major and natural minor scales are sometimes called the *Ionian* and the *Aeolian* modes.

Dorian   Phrygian   Lydian   Mixolydian

 Figure 25. The church modes

Strictly speaking, just using the notes of one of these scales does not make a tune really modal. If you want to write a modal melody yourself it is important to cadence to its tonic — just as you need to do when distinguishing b minor from D major. You can emphasize the tonic and dominant degrees by thinking of them as melodic destinations or stopping points. Phrases or sections will usually end on either the dominant or the tonic.

The Dorian mode is probably the most familiar to our ears. The only difference between Dorian and natural minor is the sixth degree, which is a half step higher in Dorian. The asterisk marks the occurence of that sixth degree in this well-known traditional song:

Are   you   go- ing   to   Scar- bor- ough   Fair,   Par- sley,   sage,   rose-   ma- ry   and   thyme,

 Figure 26. A Dorian melody

Transposing the Church modes

The pattern of steps of each of these can be transposed to any starting note, in which case it is convenient to use a key signature. For example, Dorian transposed to begin on F would use a key signature of three flats. Think this way: Dorian in its original position starts on D but uses the key signature of the C major scale, which is a major second lower . So when transposed to F it would use the key signature of the major scale a major second lower from F: E♭. In the same way, Phrygian uses the key signature of the major scale located a major third below its tonic; Lydian, a perfect fourth below; Mixolydian, a perfect fifth below.

Chromatic vs. Diatonic Scales

If you write a scale that is all half steps you'll find that you need to include some *chromatic* half steps—half steps in which the letter name does not change, such as F to F♯. That is why a scale made of all half steps is often called the *chromatic scale* (another name is the *twelve-tone scale*). *Diatonic scales* use only whole tones and *diatonic* half steps in which the letter name changes, such as E to F or G♯ to A (for more explanation of these terms see the glossary entry for *genera*).

The spelling of the half steps in a chromatic scale is variable, except that B-C and E-F are almost always spelled diatonically. The below arrangement is one possibility:

 Figure 27. A chromatic scale

 Launch the Textbook Activity 6.2. *Spelling Scales* to confirm your knowledge of the basic major and minor scales. If you want to attempt such feats as transposing modes, find *Scales* in the Activities Folder and try level 4.

Summary, Chapter VI

1. The degrees of the scale are named, in ascending order, *tonic, supertonic, mediant, subdominant, dominant, submediant, subtonic.*

2. The *natural minor scale* corresponds to the pattern of white keys beginning on A, making the pattern W H W W H W W.

3. A *key signature* tells you which scale was used to compose a piece of music; it is a collection of flats or sharps that will be used throughout the piece unless canceled briefly by a natural sign or replaced by another key signature.

4. You can identify the key of a piece by this trick: the last sharp in a sharp key signature is the seventh note of the major scale that uses that signature. In a flat key signature the last flat is the fourth note of the major scale using that signature (or, if there are two or more flats in the signature, the penultimate flat is the tonic note).

5. The *relative minor* of a major scale is the minor scale that starts on the major scale's submediant degree. The relative minor uses the same key signature as its relative major.

6. The *parallel minor* of a major scale is the minor scale that shares the same tonic. The parallel minor never has the same key signature as its parallel major.

7. The *circle of fifths* illustrates this principle: starting at C, when the tonic rises a fifth, a sharp is added to the key signature. Going downward from C, when the tonic drops a fifth, a flat is added to the signature.

8. Any natural, sharp, or flat sign that appears in a melody marks a note that is not part of the prevailing major scale or natural minor scale represented by the key signature. Sharps, flats, or naturals used within a measure are known as *accidentals* and are in effect only until the end of the measure. A *precautionary accidental* is an accidental that isn't necessary except as a reminder to the reader that an accidental in one of the previous bars is no longer in effect.

9. The *harmonic minor scale* is the same as the natural minor except that the seventh degree is raised one half step to provide a *leading tone* back to the tonic. The raising is always accomplished by use of accidentals; it is not indicated in the key signature.

10. The *melodic minor scale* is the same as the harmonic minor except that the sixth degree is also raised, to eliminate the augmented second found between the sixth and seventh degrees of the harmonic minor. The melodic minor is usually represented as reverting to natural minor when descending, though in practice the three forms of minor are freely mixed together.

11. The *pentatonic scale* is used extensively in folk music all over the world. It has five notes, which are arranged like the black keys of a piano: whole step, whole step, minor third, whole step, minor third. It is like a major scale without the fourth and seventh degrees. The pentatonic also comes in minor forms, such as: minor third, whole step, whole step, minor third, whole step.

12. The *whole-tone scale* is composed entirely from whole steps. It has only six notes and does not have a clear tonic.

13. The *octatonic scale* is an eight-tone nontraditional scale formed from alternating whole and half steps.

14. The *blues scale* is like the major scale but with ambiguous third and seventh degrees, which tend to be minor in a melody but major in the accompaniment. A blues melody often slides between the minor and major forms of the third and seventh degrees.

15. The *church modes* are predecessors of our modern major and minor scales. The pattern of steps for each mode can be found in the white keys of the piano: the mode beginning on D is the *Dorian*, E is the tonic for the *Phrygian*, F for the *Lydian*, and G for the *Mixolydian*. Our major and natural minor scales are sometimes called the *Ionian* and *Aeolian* modes.

16. The *chromatic scale* is composed of half steps. It gets its name from the fact that some of these must necessarily be *chromatic half steps*, half steps in which both notes have the same letter name, such as C to C♯. A *diatonic* half step is one in which the letter name changes, such as E-F or G♯-A. The major and minor scales and the modes are called *diatonic scales* for this reason: they include only diatonic half steps.

VII. TRIADS

The Origins of Triadic Harmony

Now that you understand consonance and dissonance and how to classify intervals it's possible to discuss *harmony*—the art of combining simultaneous pitches. We'll use the term *chord* to refer to a combination of three or more different pitch classes, and keep the term *interval* for combinations of only two pitch classes.

The type of harmony we are studying, the harmony that underlies both music of the classical era and popular music of today, is called *tonal harmony*. It is based on a type of chord called the *triad*. A triad is formed by combining the intervals of the fifth and the third; in its simplest form it looks like two thirds stacked together, as at left.

Figure 1. Major triad on C

Triads arise naturally whenever you try to make three different pitches agree with each other. It is a unique structure: *a major or minor triad (see below) is the only possible group of three notes in which all are different pitch classes and all are consonant with each of the others.* That is why the triad has come to have such importance in tonal harmony, which depends on the resolution of dissonance by consonance: consonant triads provide that resolution.

The Major and Minor Triads

Consonant triads are composed of a major third and a minor third, which add up to a perfect fifth. If the major third is the lower of the two, the triad is called a *major triad*, and if the minor third is in the lower position then the triad is a *minor triad*:

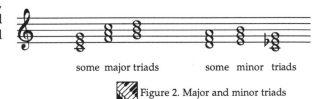

some major triads   some minor triads

Figure 2. Major and minor triads

Parts of a Triad

The note that the triad is built on is called its *root*. The triad's middle and upper notes are called its *third* and its *fifth*, named after the intervals they form with the root. In the above examples the roots of the major triads are C, F, and G, and the roots of the minor triads are D, E, and C. A triad is identified by its root and by its quality, so the first three of the above examples could be called C major, F major, and G major triads. The last three would be d minor, e minor, and c minor triads.

Open the Textbook Activity titled *7.1. Building Triads*. You'll be asked to form major or minor triads on various roots in different keys, and Practica Musica can show you the answers if you have trouble.

Dissonant Triads: Diminished and Augmented

The triad B D F is said to be *diminished* because its fifth is diminished rather than being perfect like the fifths of the major and minor triads. The diminished triad consists of two minor thirds. To label a diminished triad we use lower-case letters, since it is based on minor thirds, and we add the symbol "°" to indicate the diminished quality.

The diminished fifth is a dissonant, unstable interval, and so the diminished triad is also dissonant: because of its unstable nature it doesn't work well as a conclusion or as a point of rest—it doesn't sound "finished."

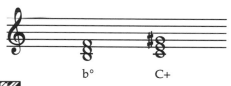

You can also make an *augmented triad*, though it is not used as often. The augmented triad is composed of two major thirds, which together form an augmented fifth. The augmented fifth sounds like a minor sixth on a piano, but it is technically dissonant (remember that "dissonance" refers to musical instability, not to unpleasantness). The chord is labeled in upper-case numerals with a "+" to show the augmentation.

 Figure 3. Diminished and augmented triads

Triads Natural to the Major Keys

The seven triads that can be made from the notes of a single major scale define the harmonic world of that key. We say they are the natural triads of a given key when they consist solely of the unaltered scale notes of that key. These seven triads are identified by the name of their scale degree (tonic, dominant, subdominant, etc.) or by the number of their scale degree in Roman numerals. We use upper and lower-case Roman numerals to distinguish major from minor triads. For instance, in a major scale the triad built on the first note is called the tonic triad, or I, the triad built on the fourth note is called the subdominant triad or IV; the submediant triad is the minor triad vi. The triad on a major key's seventh degree is always diminished and uses lower-case numerals plus the diminished symbol.

 Figure 4. Triads natural to C major

The Primary Triads in Major Keys

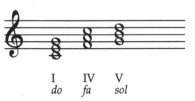

I   IV   V
do   fa   sol

Figure 5. Primary triads in major

As you can see from the upper-case Roman numerals, only three of the chords natural to the major scale are major: the ones built on I, IV, and V. The tonic, subdominant, and dominant triads are the most important chords in tonal music. Many folk and pop songs use only I, IV, and V, and the same is true of many of the best-known classical themes. We call these three the *primary triads*.

The Secondary Triads in Major Keys

The remaining triads of the key, the ones built on the second, third, sixth, and seventh degrees, provide variety and complexity. We call them the *secondary triads*:

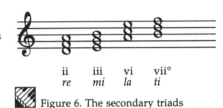

ii   iii   vi   vii°
re   mi   la   ti

Figure 6. The secondary triads

No matter what major key you are in, the primary and secondary triads always have the same qualities. As long as you use only the notes defined by the key signature, then the I, IV, and V triads will always be major, the ii, iii, and vi triads will always be minor, and the vii chord will always be diminished.

I   IV   V   I   IV   V

Figure 7. Primary triads in different keys

Triads Natural to the Minor Keys

If you build triads on each degree of a natural minor scale, again using only the notes of the scale, the quality of each chord will of course be different from what it was in the major keys. The primary triads, for example, will be minor instead of major, while three of the four secondary triads are now major. Here are the triads natural to the a minor scale:

i   ii°   III   iv   v   VI   VII

Figure 8. Triads natural to the minor scale

Altering the Minor Dominant Chord

The dominant chord doesn't work very well if it's minor. The function of a dominant chord, as we'll see later, is to lead strongly back to the tonic, and for that it is necessary that the dominant chord contain the scale's leading tone — the note a half step below the tonic. To provide the leading tone necessary for a strong dominant, composers usually raise the third of the minor dominant chord, making it major like the dominant in the major keys.

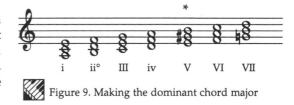

i   ii°   III   iv   V   VI   VII

Figure 9. Making the dominant chord major

This is the origin of the harmonic minor scale: the alteration made to the dominant chord raises the seventh degree of the scale, allowing more effective harmony. This alteration is always accomplished with an accidental — not by adding to the key signature.

Sometimes what is needed is not a sharp but a natural, as follows:

i   ii°   III   iv   V   VI   VII

Figure 10. Sometimes a natural is required

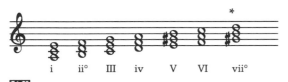

i   ii°   III   iv   V   VI   vii°

Figure 11. Other effects of a raised seventh degree

When the seventh degree is raised it can affect other chords, too. It can turn the VII chord into a vii° chord like the one in the major keys (figure 11).

Chord Inversions

So far we've presented every triad with its root in the lowest position. That is called *root position*. But the root does not have to be the lowest note. If the triad's *third* is the bass, the chord is said to be in *first inversion*. If we put the *fifth* in the bass, the chord will be in *second inversion*.

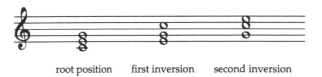

root position   first inversion   second inversion

Figure 12. Inversions of a major triad

Figured Bass (Thoroughbass)

In the 17th and 18th centuries composers often used a sort of shorthand to notate harmonic accompaniment. They provided a bass line — just the lowest notes of the accompaniment — with numbers underneath each note that indicated the required harmony. The keyboard player improvised the rest, filling in chords and decorating them, much as a jazz artist might do today.

The bass line with numbers was called a *figured bass* or *thoroughbass,* and although it is no longer used by composers we still use its figures in labeling chords, particularly inverted ones.

Figured bass works this way: each number appearing with the bass line refers to an interval needed in the harmony, as measured from the bass note. The performer is free to add octaves to the interval. The figures are often abbreviated. A 5/3 (root position triad) is assumed if no number appears. For the 6/3 (first inversion triad) only the 6 is written. For the second inversion triad, however, both intervals are specified: 6/4.

Here is an example of a simple bass line with figures.

 Figure 13. A bass line with figures

Translating the numbers into actual harmonies is called *realizing* the figured bass:

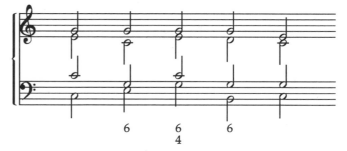

 Figure 14. A simple realization of the figures

 Open the Textbook Activity 7.2. *Recognizing Triads* for practice in recognizing the different triads. You'll be presented with triads that are sometimes in root position and sometimes inverted.

Altered Chords in Figured Bass

A flat or sharp prefix in figured bass means to use an accidental to alter the chord. A sharp or flat appearing alone in the figured bass without a number is assumed to be an abbreviation for a sharp third or flat third. So, for example, a composer using figured bass in a minor key could indicate a root position dominant chord altered to major simply by writing the root note with a "♯" underneath it.

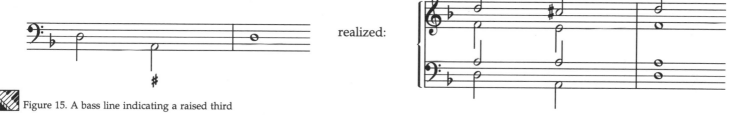

realized:

Figure 15. A bass line indicating a raised third

Figured bass can get much more complex than this, but for those of us who are not specialists in the performance of early music the simplest numbers are enough: they are used in conjunction with Roman numerals for music analysis. We use the abbreviated numbers—no figure for a root position triad and the figures 6 and 6/4 for the first and second inversions (a few others will be added when we discuss seventh chords). For example, the label "IV6" indicates a first inversion subdominant triad.

The figured bass numbers should not be confused with a practice common in popular music where, for example, a C major triad with an "A" added to it is called a "C6" chord (since the A is a sixth above the C). If you see a "6" after a letter name in a popular song or jazz book it will probably be referring to this "added-sixth chord" and not to a first inversion triad. Pop and jazz musicians don't use figured bass symbols; they specify a chord inversion by listing the bass note as part of the chord name. C/E, for example, in a pop or jazz score would be a C chord in first inversion, with E in the bass.

Voicing

The four-voice chords in the above realizations are harder to recognize than the earlier illustrations of triads, because we have repeated pitches, changed the order of the upper notes, and transposed some by octaves. All these changes are part of *voicing* a chord. Changes in voicing affect the chord's sonority but make no difference to its name or its inversion. We'll examine chord voicing in more detail, considering doubling and the use of open and close positions.

Doubling

Vocal harmony is often in four parts. To make a four-part voicing of a triad it is of course necessary to double (repeat) one of the pitch classes. The usual choice is to double the root. Next best is the fifth, and then the third. The third of a major triad is not often doubled.

It is also possible to leave out the fifth and still give the general impression of a triad, though it is incomplete. The root, of course, cannot be omitted without changing the nature of the chord, and the third is necessary to provide the chord's major or minor quality.

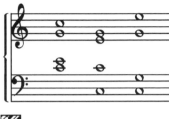

Figure 16. Doubling

Uses of Close and Open Position

Chords displayed at the beginning of this chapter were all in *close position*, with the upper notes as close to each other as possible. If the upper notes of a chord are spread out to cover a wider range they are said to be in *open position*. Vocal music for mixed voices must generally use harmonies in open position so that the voices can be in their customary range: the soprano's melody, for example, must be considerably higher than that of the tenor. All of the chords in figure 17 are C major:

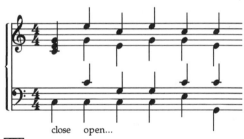

close   open...

Figure 17. Close and open position chords

In piano and orchestra scoring open voicing serves both to meet range requirements and to improve clarity. It is common to voice chords so that narrow intervals are not found in the bass. Small intervals low in pitch tend to sound "muddy." In other words, the lower parts tend to be voiced more open, as in these voicings of an F major triad.

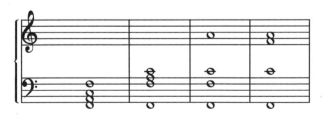

 Figure 18. Voicing for clarity   "muddy" voicing   clearer...   clearer still

Broken or Arpeggiated Chords

Triads and other chords do not always appear as above, with all the notes simultaneous. The notes of a chord are often broken: played successively rather than all at once. Bach's *Prelude in C* consists entirely of broken chords, which also serve as melody:

Figure 19. From J.S. Bach: *The Well-Tempered Clavier*

In classical piano music you will often see accompaniment chords broken into patterned figures called the *Alberti bass,* after the 18th-century composer who supposedly invented it. Here is part of Mozart's famous C major piano sonata, K. 545:

  Figure 20. Alberti bass

The word *arpeggio* describes chord notes played successively in ascending or descending order. It derives from the way harpists or guitarists sound a chord by drawing a finger across the strings:

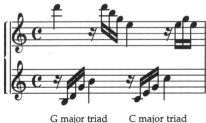

 Figure 21. Arpeggiated chords

G major triad   C major triad

Here are more examples of the many ways that chords can be varied to make an accompaniment:

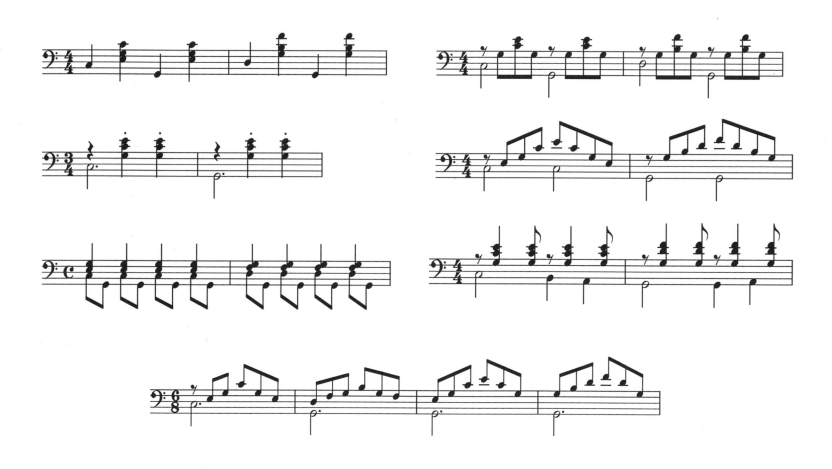

Figure 22. Chords in accompaniment

Summary, Chapter VII

1. The *triad* is the basis of tonal harmony. The major and minor triads are the only chords whose notes are mutually consonant. A triad is built by stacking two thirds together; its outer notes are a fifth apart.

2. A *major triad* is a major third with a minor third on top; a *minor triad* is a minor third plus a major third. The other triads are dissonant: a *diminished triad* is two minor thirds and an *augmented triad* is two major thirds.

3. The notes of a triad may be rearranged in *inversions* without changing the basic nature of the chord. The original arrangement as two thirds stacked together is called *root* position. If the third is placed in the bass that makes the *first inversion*; if the fifth is the bass then you have a *second inversion*. The order of the upper notes does not affect the inversion.

4. If you *double* (repeat) any of the notes of a triadic chord, the best one to double is the root. Next best is the fifth.

5. The fifth may sometimes be left out of a triadic chord, but the root and third are essential.

6. The chords of a given key are often referred to by the Roman numeral of the scale degree that they are built on (i.e., their root). Major or augmented chords are written with upper-case Roman numerals; minor or diminished chords receive the lower case. Diminished chords are further identified by the symbol "°" and augmented ones by "+." The *primary triads* are the triads built on the tonic, dominant, and subdominant degrees of a major or minor scale. All the others are called *secondary triads*.

7. The primary and secondary triads have different qualities in a minor key: i, ii , III, iv, v, VI, VII. The v is customarily converted to a major triad, V, so that it will move strongly to the tonic as it does in a major key. If the V is changed in this way the VII will also be changed to vii°. This alteration is accomplished with accidentals, not by changes in the key signature.

8. Numbers borrowed from the old practice of figured bass are often used in identifying chord inversion. A "6" added to a Roman numeral means "first inversion triad." "6/4" means a second inversion triad. The numbers refer to the intervals that notes of the chord form with the bass note, disregarding octaves. Outside the context of Roman numeral analysis, however, such as in jazz or pop music, a "6" might be intended to refer to the chord of the added sixth, such as C6.

9. Triadic chords are fundamental to all tonal music, but they may not appear in simple block form. Often they are outlined by a melody or broken into accompaniment patterns like the *Alberti bass*, or *arpeggiated* (played as a harp might play them).

VIII. ADDING TO THE TRIAD

Seventh Chords

The major and minor triads are consonant and stable; they seem to be at rest. The diminished and augmented triads are dissonant and therefore restless; they imply movement.

That desirable sense of instability is produced whenever dissonant notes are included in harmony. One dissonance that is particularly common is the interval of a seventh formed with a chord's root. This seventh can be seen as an extension of the basic structure of the triad — it's another third added above the two that form the triad. The four notes together make a *seventh chord*.

Figure 1. Some seventh chords in root position

The Dominant Seventh Chord

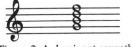
Figure 2. A dominant seventh chord built on G

The seventh that appears most often in tonal harmony is a minor seventh added to the dominant triad; the triad built on the dominant scale degree. This sonority can be seen in general terms as a major triad with a minor third on top, and so it is sometimes called the *major-minor seventh chord*. Because of its dominant function it is more often called the *dominant seventh chord*. In the major scale, it occurs naturally (i.e., without using accidentals) only on the dominant degree.

Observe that by adding a seventh to the dominant triad we have actually introduced two dissonances: the seventh between the outer notes and a diminished fifth between the seventh and the third. Figure 3 shows all of the intervals contained within the dominant seventh.

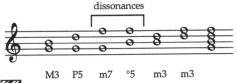

Figure 3. Dissonance in the dominant seventh

If we voice the chord differently these dissonances may change names: the minor seventh may invert to a second, for example. But the effect of instability will be the same because an inverted dissonance is still dissonant (figure 4).

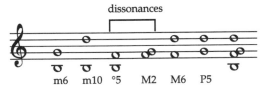

Figure 4. Revoiced seventh chord

Resolving Chordal Dissonance

As mentioned earlier, in traditional tonal music a dissonant interval *resolves* to a consonance. This is also true of the dissonant intervals in seventh chords, where the conventions of dissonance resolution have interesting consequences. Conventional resolutions follow these principles: 1) the upper note of a seventh usually moves downward by a step; 2) a second often expands to form a third, usually by moving its lower note downward; 3) a diminished interval will often contract to the nearest consonance, and 4) an augmented interval will often expand to the nearest consonance. The following are some typical resolutions:

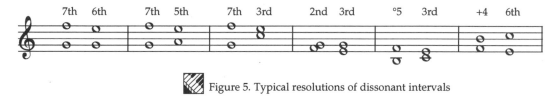

Figure 5. Typical resolutions of dissonant intervals

Suppose we apply these conventional resolutions to the dissonances within the dominant seventh chord for C major. To demonstrate we'll voice the chords with four parts, with the root doubled (figure 6).

If the seventh, which is F, moves down a step for the following chord it will be on E. If the augmented fourth, B-F, resolves by expanding to the nearest consonance it will become a sixth, E-C. What consonant triads in the key of C major would include C and E? Only the C major triad itself (I) or the a minor triad (vi).

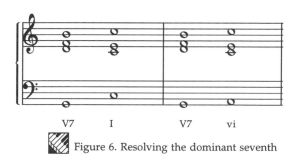

Figure 6. Resolving the dominant seventh

So we see that adding a dissonant seventh to the dominant triad, V, can create an even stronger pull toward the I or vi chords for that key. We already knew that there is a very strong relationship between the tonic and dominant degrees of the scale, and now we have a way to alter the triad built on the dominant degree so that it will reinforce that relationship. The dominant seventh chord will suggest to the ear that the next chord is going to be a tonic (or a vi, which can substitute for the tonic). The dominant seventh is a powerful means of telling the listener that a resolution to the tonic is about to happen, which is why it is unsettling if used as a final chord.

Building the Dominant Seventh in Different Keys

The dominant seventh chord is natural to all major keys. That means all four notes of the dominant seventh chord are unaltered scale notes as defined by the key signature of a major scale. Build a triad on the dominant degree of a major scale, add to it a minor seventh (which will be the subdominant degree) and you'll have a dominant seventh chord, a major triad combined with a minor seventh:

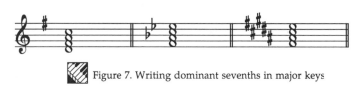

 Figure 7. Writing dominant sevenths in major keys

As we saw earlier, in minor keys the dominant chord requires an accidental to raise its third, producing a major triad with a leading tone to the tonic. Even in this case, once the chord is made major you can add a third without an accidental to make the dominant seventh chord:

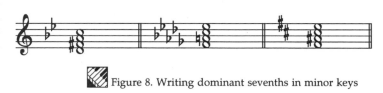

 Figure 8. Writing dominant sevenths in minor keys

Inversion of Seventh Chords

root   first   second   third

 Figure 9. Inversions of the seventh chord

Adding a fourth note to the triad allows one more inversion. If the seventh itself is in the bass position the chord is in *third inversion*.

As with triads, numbers derived from figured bass serve as abbreviations for the various inversions of seventh chords. "7" is the root position seventh chord; "6/5" means a first inversion seventh chord; "4/3" means the second inversion, and "4/2" means a third inversion. The figures again refer to intervals formed between the bass and the upper notes. As with the triads, these figures ignore octaves and doubling: a "6," for example, can refer to a sixth plus an octave.

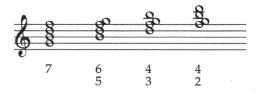

7   6   4   4
            5   3   2

 Figure 10. Figured bass for seventh chords

Notating a Second Within a Chord

As seventh chords will often include the interval of a second, you may want to know how to notate a second when writing by hand (when writing on the computer the computer will normally position the second automatically). Assuming that the notes of the second have the same stem direction, the upper note head should be written to the right of the lower one, both sharing a stem that runs between them. That stem aligns with the stem of the other chord notes. If there are any accidentals on notes of the second, they should be moved to the left so that they don't interfere with each other.

Identifying Chords Quickly

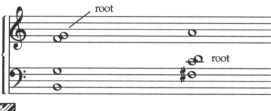

Figure 12. The upper note of a second is the chord root

It's a useful skill to be able to quickly identify the root and quality of a chord. This ability can, for example, enable you to recognize harmonies and create an accompaniment. But the roots have gotten a little harder to recognize now that we have brought in seventh chords and inversions and doublings. Here's a quick way to tell the root of any triadic chord (not counting certain jazz chords): look for seconds, sevenths, perfect fourths and fifths.

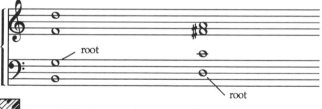

Figure 13. The lower note of a seventh is the root of the chord

If you see a second (an inverted seventh) anywhere in the chord, the chord is a seventh chord and the upper note of the second must be the chord's root (figure 12).

You may see an uninverted seventh, in which case the chord is a seventh and its lower note is the root (figure 13).

If you can see no seconds or sevenths (remember they may appear as compound intervals) then the chord must be a triad with perhaps some doubled notes. In that case the root will be the upper note of any perfect fourth you can find, or the lower note of any perfect fifth (figure 14).

 Figure 14. Using fourths and fifths to identify the root

Other Types of Seventh Chords

Adding sevenths of different types to the basic triads, major, minor, and diminished, produces a variety of seventh chords, of which five are commonly used.

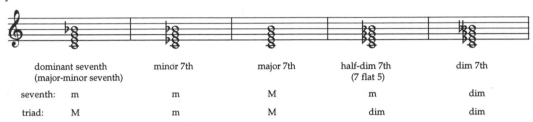

	dominant seventh (major-minor seventh)	minor 7th	major 7th	half-dim 7th (7 flat 5)	dim 7th
seventh:	m	m	M	m	dim
triad:	M	m	M	dim	dim

Figure 15.
The seventh chords

The best known of the seventh chords is the dominant seventh discussed in the previous pages, which you will recall is formed by adding a minor seventh to a major triad. That is why it is also called the "major-minor seventh."

A minor seventh added to a minor triad produces the *minor seventh chord*, which in a major key appears naturally when an unaltered seventh is added to the ii, iii, or vi chords. In minor keys it is natural to the i, iv, and v chords, though the v in minor will usually be altered to a V.

Somewhat less common, at least in classical music, is the *major seventh chord*, which results when you add a major seventh to a major triad. The major seventh chord is natural to the I and IV chords in major keys, and to III and VI in minor keys.

If a minor seventh is added to a diminished triad the result is the *half-diminished seventh chord*, called that because the fifth is diminished but the seventh is not (the half-dim 7 is also known as the "7 flat 5"). In a major key this sonority is natural only to the single diminished chord, the vii°. In a minor key it would occur in the ii°. The symbol, ⌀, can be used to label a half-dim. 7th, as in "vii⌀7."

If that seventh added to the diminished triad is lowered one half step the result is a *diminished seventh chord*, which is made entirely of minor thirds, with the outer notes separated by a diminished seventh. This seventh chord is not natural to any degree of either the major or minor scale: to form it you must add at least one accidental. The fully-diminished seventh is labeled with "°", as in "vii°7."

Open the Textbook Activity *8.1 Recognizing Seventh Chords*. This activity will help you learn to identify various types of seventh chords, using both sight and sound.

Chromatically Altered Chords

Chromatic alterations change one or more of a chord's tones to pitches not found in the current scale. We've already seen one in the fully-diminished seventh chord, which is not naturally found in any key. The major dominant triad in a minor key could also be considered a chromatically altered chord. Such chords are introduced to emphasize movement — the altered tone generally will resolve by half step in the following chord. The best-known of the remaining chords formed by chromatic alteration are the *Neapolitan sixth* chord and the various forms of the *augmented sixth*.

The Neapolitan Sixth

The Neapolitan chord is usually found in first inversion, so that it contains the interval of a sixth between its bass and one of the upper notes. For this reason it is usually called the Neapolitan sixth, though it can also appear in root position. It is most common in minor keys, and is usually found introducing a dominant triad. It is nothing more than a major triad, but what makes it special is that its root is the lowered second degree of the scale. In a minor key the Neapolitan chord will always require one accidental, a flat or a natural on its root, as at right.

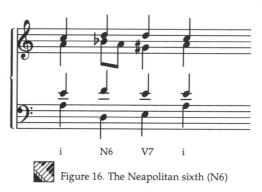

i   N6   V7   i

 Figure 16. The Neapolitan sixth (N6)

The Augmented Sixth Chords

To reach a dominant harmony a composer will sometimes choose to write dissonances that would approach the root of the dominant chord by half step from both sides at once. The sixth scale degree is lowered, bringing it to within a half step of the dominant from the upper side, and the fourth degree is raised to approach the dominant from below. The resulting interval of an augmented sixth gives the chord its name.

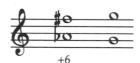

+6

Figure 17. Augmented sixth

Depending on what other notes fill out the harmony, the chord can move in various ways, either directly to the dominant chord or to the second inversion of the tonic chord, which is itself an introduction to the dominant chord. Three of the common forms of this chord have traditionally had national names, for no particular reason: the Italian, French, and German augmented sixths. The fourth is called the doubly-augmented sixth because it also contains an augmented fourth. Here are all four with their typical following chords, as they would appear in the key of C major (following page):

Ger.+6, V   Fr.+6, V   It.+6, V   ++4+6, I $\frac{6}{4}$

 Figure 18. The augmented sixth chords

Ninth Chords and Beyond

If you continue to stack thirds on the basic triad you can produce chords that include ninths, elevenths, or even thirteenths. These sonorities are not really acknowledged as such in traditional music theory, though they are essential to jazz. One reason traditional tonal theory does not explain chords above the seventh is that it has other ways to refer to the same effects. A ninth or an eleventh, for example, may appear in a work by Mozart, but the composer did not consider it to be part of a chord — it was a dissonant tone (this is the same way the "seventh chord" came into being, as a dissonance added to a triad).

The main difference between the historical and contemporary use of such chords is that they are now often treated as sounds to be heard for their own sake rather than as dissonant preparations for consonant chords. So a jazz player, or a modern symphonist, does not necessarily resolve the seventh or the other dissonances as a musician from an earlier era would have done. On the other hand, jazz musicians are still likely to follow traditional principles of voice-leading in other respects — keeping economy of motion, for example (see chapter 13).

The only simple guidelines that can be provided here for the use of chords beyond the seventh are these: they are usually played in root position, and if any notes must be left out you should at least include the root, the third, and the seventh (though a jazz pianist may want to leave the root for the bass player). That is really just the same as traditional practice, where the fifth is the most dispensible note in a chord. For example, a thirteenth chord could be reduced to four parts as at right:

 Figure 19. C 13 reduced to four voices

Non-tertian Chords

In the modern era, composers have constructed *non-tertian* chords— chords built from intervals other than the third— based on the fifth, the fourth, or even the second. These are not part of the language of classical tonal music, and generally could be said to have a coloristic rather than a harmonic function. The most popular non-tertian harmonies are chords built of fourths and fifths, which are known respectively as quartal and quintal chords (figure 19).

Fig. 20. Quintal and quartal chords

It is not always easy to avoid the tertian sound: chords built of fifths may tend to sound like tertian harmonies with every other note missing. A quartal chord with only three notes may give the impression of being really a seventh chord with a fourth substituted for its third (what a jazz player would call a "7 sus 4"). To be perceived as non-tertian, such harmonies probably need to be placed in a context where the listener does not expect tertian chords.

Open Textbook Activity *8.2. Building Seventh Chords* for practice in creating seventh chords on different roots. Practica Musica can show you the correct answer if you're not sure.

Summary, Chapter VIII

1. Seventh chords are triads with another third added to the stack. Because the interval of a seventh is dissonant, all types of seventh chords are unstable and are used in tonal music to give a sense of motion.

2. The *dominant seventh* is the most common type of seventh chord, formed by adding a minor seventh to a major triad.

3. Seventh chords have one more possible inversion: if the seventh itself is in the bass the chord is in the *third inversion*. Inversions of seventh chords are represented in analysis by these figures: root position: 7; first inversion: 6/5; second inversion: 4/3; third inversion: 4/2.

4. To quickly identify the root of an unknown chord, look first for any seconds or sevenths. If you see either one (they may be compound) the chord is a seventh chord and its root is the upper note of the second or the lower note of the seventh. If there are no seconds or sevenths in the chord, again including compound ones, then look for fifths or fourths: the upper note of the fourth or the lower note of the fifth will be the root.

5. The five seventh chords in common use are the dominant seventh described above, the *minor seventh* (a minor seventh added to a minor triad), the *major seventh* (a major seventh added to a major triad), the *half-diminished seventh* (a minor seventh added to a diminished triad), and the *fully-diminished seventh* (a diminished seventh added to a diminished triad).

6. The *Neapolitan chord* is a major triad whose root is the lowered second degree of the scale. It is usually found in first inversion, usually in minor keys, and usually moves to the dominant chord.

7. The *augmented sixth chords* are chromatically altered forms of the ii and IV chords; they are built around the interval of an augmented sixth on the lowered sixth degree of the scale. The notes of the augmented sixth expand outward to resolve in the following chord to the dominant or to a substitute for the dominant, such as the second inversion of the tonic triad. There are four augmented sixth chords: the Italian, German, French, and doubly-augmented sixth.

8. Triadic harmonies can also be formed that include 9ths, 11ths, or 13ths. These are used in jazz, but they are not an explicit part of traditional theory. Some notes can be left out of these chords: the most important ones to keep are the root, third, and seventh.

9. Chords can also be built from intervals other than the third, though such harmonies are not part of the language of tonal music. The most common of these *non-tertian* chords are the *quartal* and *quintal* chords (chords built from stacked fourths or fifths).

IX. CHORD PROGRESSION

Principles of Chord Progression

The tonic and the dominant scale degrees have a very close relationship. Whether their affinity for each other is based on acoustic principles or on cultural traditions, or on both, is hard to say — but there is a certain magnetism between them. When you build triads on the tonic and dominant degrees of the scale the triads inherit that close relationship, giving a chord change from dominant to tonic a unique sense of logical resolution.

The energy possessed by the dominant-tonic chord change is at the heart of the technique that composers of tonal music use to propel a composition through a *progression* of harmonies. The technique rests both on the importance of the dominant-tonic relationship itself and on the capacity of other chord pairs to mimic that relationship.

Chord Changes with the Primary Triads

If you were asked to describe the chord change from dominant to tonic in general terms you might list these features:

(1) The root of the second chord is a fourth above (or a fifth below) the root of the first one.

(2) The first chord is major (remember that even in a minor key we go to the trouble of altering the dominant to major).

V   I   V   I

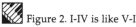
Figure 1. The dominant/tonic relationship

There are other chord changes that have one or both of these characteristics, and which consequently have some of that same energy found in the dominant-tonic pair.

The most important of these other chord changes is that from the tonic to the subdominant (i.e., from the tonic triad to the triad built on the fourth note of a major or minor scale). This is because the tonic chord's position relative to the subdominant is the same as that of the dominant to the tonic — the only difference is that the movement is away from the tonic rather than toward it.

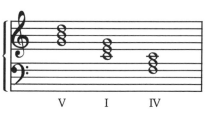

V   I   IV

Figure 2. I-IV is like V-I

The I, IV, and V chords, then, share a unique and symmetrical relationship. These three, which we earlier called the *primary triads*, are the main connecting points of a progression — the big cities, so to speak, on your harmonic highway. For much of popular music and even many well-known classical themes these are the only chords you need to know.

The power of the cycle between I, IV, and V is well illustrated in the standard twelve-bar blues progression, which works exactly the same way in hundreds of compositions.

The first line of a blues tune stays mostly on the tonic chord, with a side trip to the subdominant:

I   IV   I
Well I'm goin' away, baby, I won't be back 'till fall

The second line (using the same text) begins with the subdominant and then returns to the tonic:

IV   I
Well I'm goin' away, baby, I won't be back 'till fall

The third line finally reaches the dominant, which is usually a dominant seventh chord, and then delays return to the tonic by interjecting a subdominant again:

V7   IV   I
And if I find me a new love, I won't be back at all

Figure 3. A blues progression using I, IV, and V

Adding a new dominant after "I won't be back at all" takes us back to the beginning of the cycle, which can repeat indefinitely. Because of the regular cycle of chord changes the musicians can make considerable innovations in melody and accompaniment without losing even inexperienced listeners.

The blues progression illustrates the tension between predictability and surprise that is at the heart of effective musical structures. The conventions of the progression provide a framework for innovation, and also establish a model of predictable behavior that can be altered from time to time with great effect. Perhaps the most important of these conventions in tonal music is the journey from the tonic to the dominant and back again.

Compare the blues progression to the beginning of Mozart's *Piano Sonata in C*:

 Figure 4. I, IV, and V in a Mozart Piano Sonata

This does sound different. But Mozart's piece is still based on the same logical interplay between the three strongest chords: tonic, subdominant, and dominant. Harmonically, the two examples have much in common, at least in the first few measures.

Open the Textbook Activity *9.1. Recognizing Primary Chords*. Practica Musica will help you learn to recognize these essential chords in four-part writing. Don't stop until you pass! With a secure understanding of I, IV, and V the rest of this chapter will make better sense to you.

Harmonic Rhythm

You may have noticed that the chords in both the above examples change much less frequently than the notes do. This is true of most tonal music based on accompanied melody: we say that it tends to have *slow harmonic rhythm*. In most pieces, the underlying chord—the one that "goes with" the melody—will change only once a measure or at the most, twice, unless the piece is very slow.

J. S. Bach's famous *chorales*, short vocal works for four voices, are often studied for their harmony. The chorales could be said to have a fast harmonic rhythm, since they change chords on almost every beat:

 Figure 5. J.S. Bach: *Herzlich lieb hab ich dich, o Herr*

Extending the Dominant-Tonic Relationship

The idea that chords follow each other well if their roots are a fourth apart can be extended to the secondary triads. None of these changes has quite the strength of V-I or even I-IV, since they all begin with minor chords, but they still have a trace of that dominant-tonic relationship. For example, ii moves very nicely to V, iii to vi, and vi to ii. You can even string together a chain of such chords, as in this tune learned by every beginning piano student, "Heart and Soul":

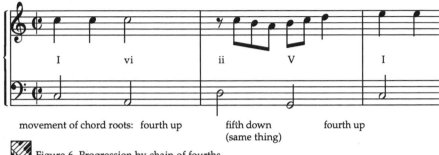

movement of chord roots: fourth up   fifth down   fourth up
                                          (same thing)

 Figure 6. Progression by chain of fourths

Progressing Backward

Though a sense of resolution is strongest with the root movement of a rising fourth/descending fifth, there is still a strong connection when the movement is by a *descending* fourth or *rising* fifth: I often moves to V, of course, and IV to I. Similarly, you may see vi-iii, ii-vi, or even V-ii, as in the Bach chorale of figure 5.

Root Movement by a Third

Another extension of the basic chord progression principle comes from the fact that triads whose roots are a third apart sound related, since they always share two notes. Of the two possible ways to move by a third, the descending direction seems to be the stronger, perhaps because ascending movement leaves the former root behind:

I   vi   I   iii

 Figure 7. Progression by thirds

The stronger descending movement can effectively be repeated at least twice in succession, as in I-vi-IV.

Chord Substitution and Root Movement by a Second

Because chords whose roots are a third apart sound so similar you can often substitute one for the other. The best example of this is the frequent use of vii° in the place of V. Another case is the "surprise" progression of V to vi, with vi substituting for the expected I (the roots of vi and I are a third apart, of course). Similarly, the IV-V could be seen as based on the very strong ii -V, with IV substituting for ii. Any case of root movement by a second can thus be explained by the basic principle of root movement by a fourth, with one chord substituting for another. I-ii, for example, is related to I-IV, with ii substituting for IV.

Until you have enough experience to feel the effectiveness of a particular progression it would probably be safer to limit root movement by a second to one change at a time, as below:

Figure 8. Progression by seconds

IV   V   I   ii

Secondary Dominants

If we want to strengthen those progressions in which the root movement imitates the rising fourth of the dominant-tonic pair, we need to make the first chord seem more like a real dominant. A dominant is always a major chord, to begin with, so we can alter minor chords to make them major. The chord ii, for example, which frequently moves to V, can be altered to II, which makes it sound like a "V of V." We call such a fake dominant a *secondary dominant* (figure 9).

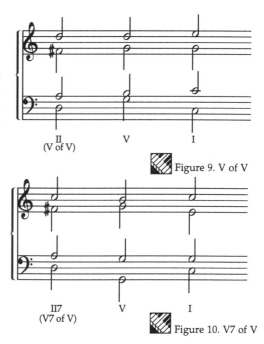

II
(V of V)   V   I

Figure 9. V of V

The secondary dominant is still more convincing if we add a minor seventh to it, making it into a dominant seventh chord (figure 10).

II7
(V7 of V)   V   I

Figure 10. V7 of V

You can convert any of the triads in a key into secondary dominants, except the IV chord in a major scale or the VI chord in a minor scale. Why can't those chords function as secondary dominants? Because there is no scale note a perfect fourth above them. For example, the IV chord in C is built on F, and a perfect fourth above F is B♭, which is not in the C scale. So there is no note in the C scale that could use F as its dominant.

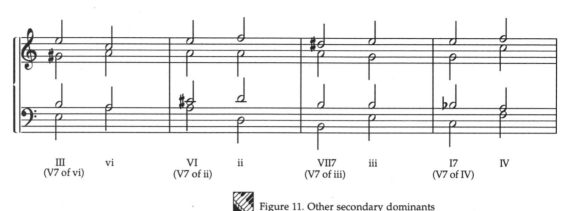

III (V7 of vi)   vi   VI (V7 of ii)   ii   VII7 (V7 of iii)   iii   I7 (V7 of IV)   IV

Figure 11. Other secondary dominants

Modulation

Secondary dominants are one means of giving the impression that the key has changed and that a new tonic has been established. If the new tonic is confirmed by further chord changes it could be said that the music has modulated to a new key. If the passage in the new key is lengthy a key signature might be displayed to mark the change, but often the change of key is accomplished using accidentals alone.

Modulation is usually made to a key that is closely related to the previous key, that is, to a key that shares some of the same chords. The composer can then modulate by *common-chord modulation*, changing the function of one of the shared chords so that, for example, I of the old key is now IV in the new key, as in figure 12.

V   iii   I   IV   I6   vi   vii°7 of vi   vi   iii   V6   I   V of V   V   V of V   V

Figure 12. Modulation (from Bach, Chorale 160)

In G: IV   V   I   V   I

The Chord Progression Game

The above principles are not intended to define all that is possible in harmony. They are a way of describing what tonal composers have usually written in simple pieces. By following these principles your music has a better chance of pleasing you in the same way that you have been pleased by other compositions.

The concepts described above can be summarized in two charts that we will call the "chord boards":

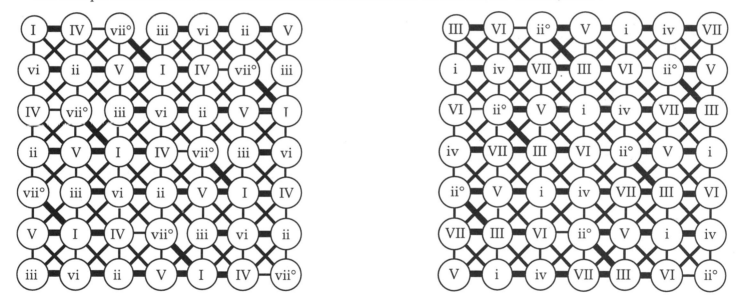

Figure 13. Chord boards for major and minor keys

The "chord boards" are for playing a sort of composition game. To play, you start with any one of the circles numbered "I" for tonic, and then you move to other circles to build a chord progression. Your last chord should be another I, preferably preceded by a V. As in most board games, you can move only in certain ways:

(1) You can move along any of the lines that connect chords. Most of the time this means you can move either horizontally, vertically, or diagonally.

(2) You can't skip over chords.

(3) You can move horizontally rightward any number of times consecutively, but in any other direction only twice consecutively.

(4) At any time you can jump to a chord of the same name (if you're on a ii spot you can jump to any other ii). This is needed if you reach an edge of the board.

(5) You can alter a chord to a secondary dominant (that is, make it major and maybe add a seventh) but if you do, it should be followed by the chord to its immediate right.

The thicker lines are an extra help; they indicate the stronger type of movement. The strong line from vii° to I shows that vii° is used like V to return to the tonic.

The chord boards take no account, of course, of the greater concerns that motivate composers, but they are a fun way to experiment with harmony.

Summary, Chapter IX

1. A series of harmonies is called a *chord progression*.

2. The powerful relationship between the dominant and the tonic chords is at the heart of all tonal chord progressions. Other chord pairs can mimic the tonic-dominant relationship and so give impetus to a progression, even when the first of the two is minor. Consequently, the strongest type of chord movement is that in which the roots of the two chords are separated by a fourth or fifth, as they are in the tonic-dominant pair, — especially a rising fourth or descending fifth.

3. The *primary triads* are the tonic, dominant, and subdominant chords. These share a unique and symmetrical relationship wherein the tonic has the same relationship to the subdominant as the dominant has to the tonic. These three are the most important chords in a standard progression. Chords a third down from the tonic and subdominant are sometimes substituted for them: vi for I; ii for IV.

4. Chords usually change at a relatively slow pace. Most often they change no more than twice in a measure; occasionally they will not change at all for several measures. The speed of the chord changes is called the *harmonic rhythm*.

5. As a general rule, root movement of a rising fourth or descending fifth is strong and effective and may be repeated without limit; other kinds of root movement should not be repeated more than twice successively.

6. If a progression involves root movement of a rising fourth/descending fifth the relationship between the two chords can be made even stronger by making the first one into a *secondary dominant*. This is done by altering the chord (if it needs it) to make it major and perhaps also by adding a minor seventh to make a "dominant seventh" chord. The result mimics the relationship between the dominant and tonic. If a chord is altered in this way it is referred to as "V (or V7) of x," where x is the second chord. The ii chord, for example, can be made into "V of V."

X. BUILDING MELODY

No one has ever been able to adequately describe what makes a great melody. Yet we can list some superficial characteristics that are shared by good melodies, and these may at least help you to make tunes that are not awkward. We'll examine several melodies and discuss the way that each moves, how its ideas are organized into *phrases*, and how it implies an underlying chord progression. In chapter 11 we'll discuss how the ideas in a melody are extended and developed.

Melodic Movement

Great and memorable melodies are often ones that are easy to sing, even if they are meant to be played by an instrument. Perhaps we find a tune more enjoyable if we can imagine singing it —or perhaps the qualities that make something easy to sing are also valuable aesthetically. This famous melody from Brahms' First Symphony, for example, could easily be a song with words although it was written to be played by an orchestra:

 Figure 1. Theme from Finale of Brahms' Symphony No. 1

We could begin by thinking about the characteristics that make a melody easy to sing. The excerpt from Brahms will serve as a good example.

First, Brahms' melody has a limited *range*. In other words, it never gets very far away in pitch from where it started. The excerpt above is confined to the notes within a seventh. Most famous melodies stay within an octave, or at most an octave plus a third or fourth.

Second, the movement is mostly by step, with some small *leaps* (a leap is defined as any interval larger than a second). No leap in this melody is larger than a fifth, and even that leap marks a dividing point in the tune (measure 4). If you would like your melody to have a similar flowing quality be sure to use mostly stepwise movement, with occasional small leaps. Melodies with mostly stepwise movement are called *conjunct*, those with many large leaps are *disjunct*. Most successful melodies are conjunct.

Third, leaps larger than a fourth tend to be *compensated* by an immediate move in the other direction, and in most great melodies leaps larger than a fifth or at most a sixth are rare unless they are octaves. Even when the leap is small, singable melodies rarely leap twice in a row in the same direction, *unless the notes involved are all part of the same triad.*

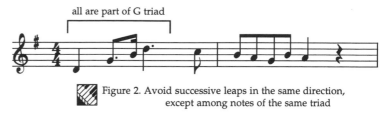

 Figure 2. Avoid successive leaps in the same direction, except among notes of the same triad

Fourth, all intervals in the Brahms melody are major or minor or perfect — there are no augmented or diminished intervals. Use of an augmented or diminished interval in a melody is not unknown, but it is unusual, and it is more difficult for a singer.

Finally, the rhythm of a great tune tends to be fairly simple. A melody with many fast notes is difficult to sing, as are rhythms with many stops and starts. A general rule for melodic rhythm is this — could you imagine singing words to it? If not, maybe it won't work very well even without words.

You might compare the examples below. The first is the beginning of "My Country, 'Tis of Thee." The second example has the same meter and the same number of notes, but it moves in ways that violate the above principles. It would be very difficult to sing and probably would not appeal to many listeners. Roughly speaking, the second one "jumps around too much."

 Figure 3. "My Country, 'Tis of Thee" (melody from "God Save the King")

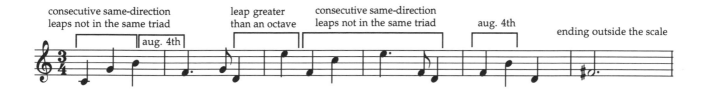

Figure 4. An unsuccessful melody with the same rhythm

Repetition

A good melody is more than just something that is singable. If a great melody could be written by merely following the above rules then even Practica Musica could write one — but the tunes invented by Practica Musica seem to wander around in a pleasant way without really saying anything meaningful (sometimes they will sound meaningful, but if so, it's just good luck). Perhaps we should compare the Brahms melody with one invented by the computer, to see if we can discover why the first sounds meaningful and the other is only amusing.

Below is a tune invented by Practica Musica. It follows the above rules for melodic movement, but it is not likely to give competition to Brahms. Is there anything specific you could name that the Brahms melody has and this one lacks?

 Figure 5. A melody invented by Practica Musica

One big difference is that the machine-made melody has no *repetition*, whereas the last four measures of the Brahms are almost the same as the first four. The sections labeled *A* are identical; *B* and *B'* are almost the same:

 Figure 6. Repetition in the Brahms melody

"My Country, 'tis of Thee" also includes two measures that closely resemble others:

Figure 7. Repetition in "My Country, 'Tis of Thee"

Music depends a great deal on repetition. Listening to a piece of music is a little like hearing a story told in a new language whose words are taught to you as you go along. The teaching is done through repetition of melody fragments, of chord progressions, of whole sections.

Often the repetition is not exact: it may involve some kind of variation or development of the original idea. The fourth measure of the Brahms tune is slightly varied when it returns, and the third and fourth measures of "My Country, 'tis of Thee" represent a more extensive variation or development of the idea that formed the first two measures. In both tunes this development of a previous idea helps to give the listener the impression that the melody is a unified whole rather than just a string of unrelated notes. The melody invented by Practica Musica, on the other hand, presented several "ideas" but didn't do anything with them — it just wandered on to other ideas. That shows a certain lack of appreciation for its own work, which is part of the reason why the computer is no threat to the livelihood of human composers. In chapter 11 we'll discuss various techniques a human composer uses to extend and develop melodic ideas.

The Phrase

An important characteristic of the Brahms tune is that it clearly divides into *phrases*. The musical phrase is like a phrase in language, but it is even more like a line of poetry. It is separated from the next phrase by a form of musical punctuation that has an effect much like the end of a poetic line, often producing a slight pause or the taking of a breath.

 Figure 8. Phrases in the Brahms melody

The beginning of the second phrase in the Brahms is easy to see because the second phrase is basically a repetition of the first one. If you could hear and understand the harmonies implied by the tune (you'll eventually be able to do this) you would also notice a harmonic change that marks the end of this first phrase. The tune begins on the tonic chord, passes through the subdominant, and at the end of the phrase comes to rest on the dominant. The "incomplete" feeling associated with the dominant tells the listener that more is to come. The second phrase, on the other hand, ends on a solid tonic chord, marking the end of a neat musical "statement." Such endings of phrases are sometimes called *open* and *closed* endings. The closed ending must finish on a note of the tonic chord while the open ending should finish on a different note, often one of those that make up the dominant chord.

The first two phrases of "Twinkle, Twinkle Little Star" form a pair, the first of which has an open ending and the second a closed ending:

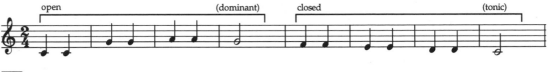

 Figure 9. Open and closed phrases in "Twinkle, Twinkle, Little Star"

The two-measure phrases that begin "My Country, 'Tis of Thee" are another open-closed pair (see figure 7).

The Period

The pair of phrases in figure 9 could be called a *period*, which is roughly analogous to a complete sentence in spoken language. A period is two or more phrases that make a natural group, the last one having a closed ending.

Cadences

The effect of an "open" ending and a "closed" one is produced by the *cadence* at the end of each phrase. A cadence is a real or implied chord change that provides a kind of harmonic punctuation at a phrase ending, just as a comma or period can end a phrase in verbal language. An open ending is produced by a cadence to the V, which is known as an *incomplete cadence* or a *half-cadence*. The more final-sounding V-I is called the *authentic cadence*, which makes a closed ending. Another final cadence is the IV-I, called the *plagal cadence* (*plagal* derives from the Greek word for "oblique" or "slanting," perhaps because a plagal cadence seems to be less solid than the authentic cadence). Authentic and plagal cadences are further classified as *perfect* if the tonic note is in the highest voice.

 Figure 10. Cadences in the Brahms melody

Harmonic Implications of Melody

Cadences have brought us to an important aspect of melody: its implied harmony. A successful melody in the tonal style will tend to suggest harmonies that make a strong chord progression according to the principles of chapter 9.

This melody seems to demand the harmony provided by Brahms, a very clear and solid progression using I, IV, and V:

 Figure 11. Implied harmony of the Brahms melody

"My Country, 'tis of Thee" also carries a chord progression that is firm and logical. It could be harmonized with just I, IV, and V, but often secondary chords and even the "V7 of vi" are added, making a strong chain-of-fourths progression:

Figure 12. Implied harmony in "My Country, 'Tis of Thee"

The harmony that is best suited to a given melody is another clue to its potential success: it is hard to imagine a successful tune that could not be harmonized with a good chord progression. Understanding how a melody implies harmony will help you to compose your own melodies, and will also enable you to harmonize an existing tune.

Harmonizing Melody

A melody may contain ambiguous places where either of two chords would serve as well, but often the implied harmony is clearly spelled out. Some melodies signal which chords underlie them by outlining those chords melodically: it's easy to tell such a melody by the fact that it moves mostly by leaps of a third. Two leaps of a third in the same direction will, of course, always spell a triad. The implied harmony in this famous work is unambiguous:

I   V7   I

 Figure 13. Successive thirds outline the harmony in this excerpt from Haydn's "Surprise" Symphony

Leaps of a fourth or a fifth or a seventh can also be part of an outlined triadic chord. This melody begins with a leap of a fourth from C to F, signaling an F major chord (remember the rule for quick recognition of chords: if you see a perfect fourth the upper note is probably the root of the chord). The last measure has a leap of a seventh and also a leap of a fifth, but both of these fit into a C7 chord, which would be the V7 chord for the key of F.

I   V7

 Figure 14. A leap of a seventh is likely to outline an implied seventh chord

Nonharmonic Tones

It is a little harder to see the chords in melodies that include notes that are not meant to be part of the harmony. Such notes are called *nonharmonic tones*, also called *nonchordal tones*. These will be discussed in more detail in chapter 13, but for the moment it is enough to know that nonharmonic tones usually move by step to a note that *is* part of the chord.

Nonharmonic tones that come in rhythmically strong positions — for example, on a metric accent or on the first part of a beat subdivision—are called *accented* nonharmonic tones. These generally move downward by step to a chord tone. Unaccented nonharmonic tones can be found moving either up or down, but again will almost always move by a step to a note that is part of the chord. So if the movement of the melody is upward by step the accented notes are probably part of the chord; if the movement is downward by step the accented notes may or may not be part of the chord, as in figure 15.

Figure 15. Recognizing harmony in a melody with nonharmonic tones. From Clementi: *Rondo*

It helps in these ambiguous cases to know that most melodies have a slow harmonic rhythm: chords will generally change only twice a bar in 4/4 or even less often. When they do change, the change will almost always occur on the notes with the strongest metric accent: the first beat of the measure, or possibly also the third beat of a 4/4 measure and the first or second beats in a 6/8 measure. In the above example the chord changes twice, both times on the strongest beat of the bar. With a typically slow harmonic rhythm a group of sixteenth notes or eighth notes moving stepwise *must* include some nonchordal tones, since you won't be able to change chords fast enough to agree with all of them. The last beat of the above could harmonize with a V chord (D major), which would make the two Gs (instead of A and F) into nonharmonic tones. However, following the principle of changing chords only when necessary and preferably on the strongest beats, the G major triad holds until the end of that bar and will change on the following downbeat.

Finally, it is essential to know the typical chord progressions. The F♯ and D in measure two of the above example could be part of the iii chord or the V, but your first guess should always be the stronger and more common progression, which in this case would be I-V. Also, you can look ahead and see that the following chord is again going to be I — and a I-V-I would make much more sense than I-iii-I.

It's interesting that two of our three principles for melody writing are closely related: the rules of movement that make a melody easy to sing have the effect of making it easier to harmonize, too. The preference for stepwise motion and for leaps that outline triads naturally allows dissonance resolution and produces a slow harmonic rhythm. This can be illustrated by attempting to apply the same principles to harmonize the "unsuccessful" melody from figure 3. The implied chords change frequently without making a very strong series. It would be hard to come up with a harmonization much better than this:

Figure 16. Implied harmony in an awkward melody

In short, melody and harmony are inseparable. The harmony grows from the melody and vice-versa; if either is poor the result is likely to be poor. While the principles described above do not assure you greatness as a melodist, they may help you to avoid the worst errors.

Open the Textbook Activity titled *10.1. Shaping melody*. This activity provides you with the rhythm of some well-known tunes and asks you to make new melodies with the same rhythm. Just enter the desired pitches in the blank staff; you'll find that the rhythmic values appear automatically. To enter notes, choose the note tool and then click in the staff or play notes on the screen keyboard or a midi instrument. To remove notes, select them with the arrow tool and press the Delete (Backspace on Windows computers) key. To change the pitch of a note already entered, drag it with the arrow tool. The sharp/flat tools above the screen piano will also change the pitch of a selected note. For example, to sharp a note, select it with the arrow tool and then click on the sharp tool.

Try to make a melody that follows the guidelines discussed in this chapter: one that stays within an octave, that moves mostly by steps, that avoids leaps larger than a sixth, that compensates any leaps of a fifth or sixth, and that avoids movement by augmented or diminished leaps such as the one from F to B. You can choose any key from the key signature box. For now it would be best to stick to the notes of the key, and end on the tonic note. You are not graded in this activity, but you can save your melody as a file, or print it.

Summary, Chapter X.

1. Memorable melodies are often ones that are easily singable, even if they are not intended to be sung.

2. Some qualities that make a tune singable are (1) range limited to an octave, (2) mostly stepwise motion (that is, the melody is *conjunct* rather than *disjunct*), (3) leaps greater than a fourth compensated by immediate movement in the opposite direction, (4) few augmented or diminished leaps, (5) simple rhythm.

3. A melodic *phrase* is generally two to four measures in length; it corresponds to a phrase of language or a line of poetry and is sometimes set off in performance by a taking of breath or a slight pause.

4. A *cadence* is the chord change that marks the end of a phrase. A I-V cadence is called an *incomplete cadence* or *half-cadence*; it produces an "open" phrase ending. The V-I cadence is called the *authentic* cadence and the IV-I the *plagal* cadence; both of these produce a "closed" phrase ending, since they end on the tonic. Phrases often come in pairs, one of which may end with an open ending and the other with a closed ending. The two together can be called a *period*.

5. A successful tonal melody will usually imply a strong chord progression with a slow harmonic rhythm.

6. To harmonize a melody, follow these principles:

   a. First, look for triads outlined by the melody notes.

   b. Then look for *nonharmonic tones* in the melody. These usually involve stepwise movement. Since two notes a step apart cannot be part of the same triad one of them will be a nonharmonic tone (for this purpose sevenths, too, are "nonharmonic tones"). *Accented* nonharmonic tones are those in rhythmically strong positions: they usually will move downward by step to a chord tone. *Unaccented* nonharmonic tones will also usually move by step to a chordal tone, but they can go up as well as down.

   c. Often two or more chords would harmonize equally well with the notes in a measure; use the chord that would make the best progression *from* the chord of the previous measure and *to* the chord that follows.

XI. DEVELOPING MELODY

Now that you have some superficial guidelines for making a melody comprehensible and easy to sing, it would be helpful to know more about how your melodic ideas can be extended and developed.

There are specific ways that a melodic idea can be varied while still keeping a recognizable connection with its former shape. Knowledge of these techniques is an important part of the composer's skill, though some of them are often used unconsciously and can even be found in many folk melodies. "Lightly Row" is a traditional children's song that illustrates techniques of melodic development:

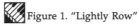Figure 1. "Lightly Row"

The Motive

The first measure of "Lightly Row" consists of a three-note pattern that appears frequently in the song — in fact, nine of the sixteen measures consist of repetitions or variations of this same small idea, which can be called a *motive*:

 Figure 2. Motive from "Lightly Row"

| motive | transposed downward | preserving rhythm and repeated notes | rhythm only |

A motive is a short, distinctive fragment of melody, or even just a rhythm, that appears repeatedly in recognizable form. Measure two of "Lightly Row" is an example of a motive varied by *transposition*, whereas measure four is a variation that preserves only the rhythm and the repeated notes of the motive. In measures ten and twelve you can find a still more distant variation that discards even the repeated notes and keeps the rhythm only.

One of the most famous motives of all time is the one Beethoven used to begin his Fifth Symphony (figure 3).

 Figure 3. Motive from Beethoven, Symphony No. 5

The motive in this case is four notes: three that repeat and one that descends a third. That pattern, sometimes reduced to just its rhythm, appears in many different forms throughout the work (figure 4).

 Figure 4. Development of the Beethoven motive

The Sequence

Of the many ways of varying a melodic idea, the most common is the *sequence*, in which the melodic phrase is repeated at a higher or lower pitch, usually beginning a second above or below the initial note. The first and second measures of "Lightly Row" form a sequence, as do measures 9-10 and 11-12.

 Figure 5. Sequence in "Lightly Row"

Sequences can be carried on as far as you like, though they tend to sound silly if they continue too long. For example, three times is pushing the limit for this idea:

Figure 6. Continuing a tonal sequence

Notice the slight changes in the intervals of the tune in figure 6. For example, the step following the dotted quarter is a minor second originally, but a major second in both of the sequences. That is because this most common type of sequence, the *tonal sequence*, uses no accidentals. If the original goes up a second then the sequence goes up a second, but without accidentals it may turn out that the second is minor instead of major, or vice-versa.

Figure 7 illustrates the *real* sequence, which preserves exactly the shape of the original melody by adding accidentals. This means that the sequence will soon move into other scales, which is usually undesirable:

Figure 7. A real sequence soon leaves the key

Launch Practica Musica and run the Textbook Activity titled *11.1. Tonal Sequencing*. You'll be presented with brief melodic ideas and asked to repeat them in a tonal transposition as you would when sequencing. The transposition will always be at the interval of a second, the most common interval for sequences. Just write a single tonal transposition of the given idea, starting on the requested note, and Practica Musica will tell you if you make a mistake.

Regular Transformations

There are four regular (i.e., mechanical) operations that can change a motive or an entire melody while maintaining a family resemblance to the original: they are *transposition, inversion, retrograde,* and *retrograde inversion.* For all of these transformations we'll consider only the tonal forms, which are the most interesting and by far the most common.

Transposition we've already seen in the sequence: the melodic idea is played at a different pitch level. Some minor intervals might become major and major ones minor, but the shape of the melody is retained.

To make an *inversion* of a melody you substitute the corresponding ascending interval for every descending interval, and vice-versa. The motive in figure 8 rises two seconds and then drops a third and a fourth, so its inversion descends two seconds and then rises a third and a fourth:

original   inversion

Figure 8. Tonal inversion

A *retrograde* variation is the reverse of the original. Sometimes only the pitches are reversed; sometimes the rhythm is reversed as well. You may recognize this retrograde segment of a well-known tune:

Figure 9. Retrograde of a portion of "yadhtriB yppaH"

Finally, you can make a variation that is both backwards and inverted: a *retrograde inversion* (same melody):

Figure 10. Retrograde inversion

Two Types of Rhythmic Variation

There are also regular changes that can be made in rhythmic patterns. Like the regular transformations of pitch patterns, these rhythmic transformations produce a variant whose connection with the original is easily recognized.

The rhythm could be made in larger values (*rhythmic augmentation*), as with this version of the Beethoven motive:

(original)   rhythmic augmentation

 Figure 11. Rhythmic augmentation

Or it could be made in shorter values (*rhythmic diminution*):

 Figure 12. Rhythmic diminution

Free Transformation: Elaboration

The regular transformations can be combined with free variation, in which pitch and rhythm are changed in less predictable ways. One type of free transformation is *elaboration*, in which extra notes are added to the melody. Sometimes the rhythms and pitches will be changed freely as well, to the point where you may scarcely recognize the original idea. You may have more trouble hearing the Beethoven motive in figure 13 (he didn't write this).

Figure 13. Elaboration

A Transformed Motive

Here is an illustration of how the above techniques can produce a great deal of music from a single idea:

original   tonal transposition   inversion   inversion + transposition   retrograde   retrograde inversion

rhythmic augmentation   rhythmic diminution   elaboration

 Figure 14. Transformations

So far we've looked at the type of movement usually found in a good melody, the way its ideas are expressed in phrases, its implied harmony, and various ways that a single small idea can be extended and developed. This first part of the task might be compared to the design of parts for a sculpture or a building. Next comes the task of building these parts into a larger structure.

Summary, Chapter XI

1. A *motive* is a small melodic or rhythmic idea that is varied and developed and extended in a composition.

2. *Sequence* is the technique of developing a brief melodic idea by transposing it up or down one or more times in succession. Usually it is transposed by a second, less frequently a third.

3. The *tonal sequence* allows the quality of melodic intervals to change according to the key (i.e., it does not use accidentals to maintain the quality of each interval). The *real sequence,* unusual in tonal music, represents an exact transposition of the original pattern and will usually require the use of accidentals.

4. The *regular transformations* are ways of mechanically changing a tune or a rhythm while maintaining a clear relationship to the original. *Transposition* repeats a pitch pattern at a higher or lower starting point; *inversion* changes the direction of each interval in the melody; *retrograde* reverses the tune, and *retrograde inversion* both inverts it and reverses it. Regular transformations of rhythm include *augmentation,* in which each note is increased in value by the same proportion, and *diminution,* in which the note values are all diminished by the same proportion.

5. *Elaboration* is the free development of a melodic idea, adding additional notes and perhaps altering the pattern in other ways.

XII. ELEMENTS OF FORM

Binary and Ternary Song Forms

We are now prepared to look again at the song "Lightly Row," this time to consider the pattern made by its phrases. A common way to study phrase patterns is to label each phrase with a letter, similar phrases being given the same letter:

Figure 1. Rounded binary form: "Lightly Row"

The phrases show the pattern *AA'BA'*. The first two phrases are a matched pair in which the first has an open ending and the second a closed ending (sometimes called an *antecedent-consequent* phrase pair). In the letter diagram the accent mark on the second *A* indicates that the two phrases have different cadences. Then follows a contrasting phrase marked *B,* which has an open ending, and finally a closed version of the *A* phrase returns to end the verse.

Many other songs and dances share this form, which is known as *rounded binary*. It's called binary (two-part) because it divides in halves, and it's "rounded" in that a portion of the first half returns at the end. As we'll see later, the return of beginning material at the end is an important principle and is found in much larger works. The return makes this almost a *ternary* (three-part) form, a clearer example of which is "Twinkle, Twinkle, Little Star" (figure 2).

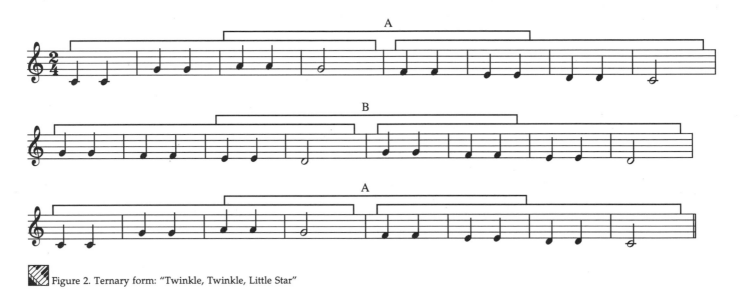

Figure 2. Ternary form: "Twinkle, Twinkle, Little Star"

If the melody of the the first phrase doesn't return, the form is simple binary, as in "Greensleeves":

Figure 3. Simple binary: "Greensleeves"

All of the above forms share one characteristic: they are built from two contrasting elements: *A* and *B*. Sometimes *A* and *B* are repeated, sometimes not; sometimes *A* returns again after *B* and sometimes it does not.

Other songs, however, are made from nothing more than a single phrase pair, such as this one:

 Figure 4: A song consisting of one period

Other Forms of Organization

Almost any simple traditional or popular song will have one of the above forms of organization, or something closely resembling one of them. However, there are also other types of musical organization based on completely different principles, and we will look at several of those next.

The Chaconne

The *chaconne,* in the time of Bach, was an instrumental piece in a slow triple meter built on a repeated chord progression. The chaconne technique survives today in much popular instrumental and vocal music in which a simple progression is repeated while the melody changes and develops. Though it is not in triple meter, "Heart and Soul" might be considered a sort of modern chaconne:

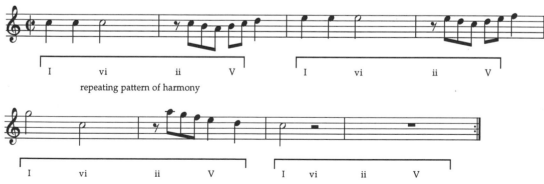

Figure 5. A modern "chaconne"

Ostinato and the Passacaglia

Strictly speaking, a chaconne repeats only the chord progression itself, while the bass melody may vary. Other pieces may repeat the bass melody exactly, forming an *ostinato bass* or *ground bass*. The word *passacaglia* , though sometimes used interchangeably with "chaconne," can specifically apply to works built on an ostinato. In Pachelbel's well-known Canon in D, which could be described as a combination canon and passacaglia, the bass player is given the task of repeating this ostinato bass fifty-seven times!

 Figure 6: The ostinato bass of Pachelbel's *Canon in D*

The other voices of the Pachelbel Canon are complicated; this simple repeating pattern in the bass helps to make the composition easier to understand.

Canon and round

One of the most enjoyable group activities for students of music is the singing of *canons* and *rounds*. A canon is a composition in which a single melody is repeated in several voices that begin at different times. Probably the best-known canon is "Row, Row, Row Your Boat," which is a special type of canon known as a *round* or *circular canon* — a canon whose ending harmonizes with its beginning and which therefore can repeat without stopping. Here's another round that works very well and which you may not know:

 Figure 7: An old English round

This round can be sung in three parts. The second singer begins when the first one reaches the "x," and the third singer begins when the second singer reaches the "x." Each singer on reaching the end goes immediately to the beginning again without missing a beat.

You can see the effect of this more clearly if we write out the first bars as they would be heard. This would be called writing the music *in score*, so that all the sounding parts can be seen together:

Figure 8: A round written in score

You can try singing this and several other rounds with the help of Practica Musica, which will gladly play two of the parts as you tap the rhythm of your own. Open the Textbook Activity titled *12.1. Rounds* and choose one of the several example rounds. By default you'll be given the first of the several parts, but you can switch to one of the other voices by clicking on any note in one of the other staves. Press the "Start" button and then tap any keys in the middle row of your computer, matching the rhythm of your part. The pitches will be supplied for you; all you need to do is read your rhythm, and the other voices will follow along. After you learn how to keep your part, try singing the round with other people (not done at many parties, but it should be).

Compound forms: The Classical Symphony

In the above examples of single forms the letters have represented just phrases. If we instead use letters to represent longer passages of music we can see how these simple formal ideas are also involved in the making of large pieces. As an example we'll discuss the classical *symphony*, a large composition for orchestra whose characteristic structure dates from the late 18th century. The symphony is typically divided into four sections or *movements*, each of which has a traditional form.

Sonata Form

The phrase structure of "Lightly Row" is a very distant relative of the plan for the first movement of most classical symphonies, which, although much more complicated, is still basically a rounded binary form in which the beginning material returns at the end.

This form, called *sonata form*, is probably more important than any other in music of the classical era. It is always used for the first movement of a sonata, and most of the works of that era are sonatas: symphonies are sonatas for orchestra, string quartets are sonatas for quartet, concertos are sonatas for a solo instrument and orchestra.

The divisions within a sonata are based on more than just similar melodies, however. The sonata is organized around its *key*, which changes in the course of each section. The first section, called the *exposition*, presents melodies in the tonic key and then *modulates* (changes key), usually to the key of the dominant. So, for example, a sonata in C major would be in G major at the end of the exposition. The next section, called the *development*, will often use some of the techniques described in chapter 11 to modify and vary the melodic material presented in the exposition, and it may also modulate to a number of other keys. The end of the development will be marked by a return of the melodies heard at the beginning, in their original key. But this *recapitulation* will be rewritten so that it doesn't modulate to the dominant — this time it will end on the tonic.

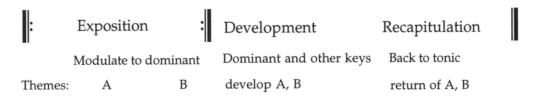

Figure 9: Sonata form

Theme and Variations

The second movement of a classical symphony is usually slow and cast in an expanded version of the binary or ternary form found in songs. Sometimes, however, a composer may choose to write a *theme and variations*. The theme, often a folk song or other well-known melody, will be played through once in its plain form and will then be played a number of additional times with various alterations. The goal of the composer is to change the music in interesting ways while still allowing the listener to recognize the theme. Though not from a symphony, the following is a particularly clear example of variation. You should be able to recognize the tune we know as "Twinkle, Twinkle, Little Star" in this excerpt:

Figure 10: From Mozart: Variations on *"Ah, vous dirai-je, Maman"*

Many sets of variations will include one in which the key is changed from major to minor or vice-versa, or in which the melody serves as an outline for a heavily elaborated version. The meter may be changed in some variations: for example, Mozart includes a triple meter variation of this duple melody. The possibilities are limited only by the imagination of the composer.

Minuet and Trio

The third movement of a classical symphony is almost always a pair of dances in triple meter, called a *minuet and trio*. The minuet and trio displays both binary and ternary form, since each dance is in rounded binary form and the movement as a whole is ternary — the trio serves as the middle section and the minuet is repeated afterward. Usually the minuet has the more vigorous dance-like rhythms, while the trio, often in a contrasting key, has a lyrical (song-like) character. A typical minuet and trio is outlined in figure 11.

Figure 11. Minuet and trio

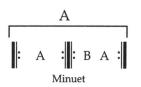
Minuet

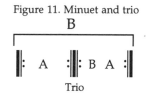
Trio

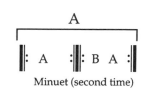
Minuet (second time)

Rondo

Finally, the last movement of the symphony may appear in *rondo* form, which resembles this: *ABACAD...A*. That pattern can be compared to a repeated ternary form, except that again each letter refers to a much larger musical passage and the *B* is constantly being replaced by new material: *C, D,* etc. The distinguishing feature of the rondo is the repeated return of the *A* material, which is usually an easily recognizable passage, the *rondo theme*. Between the first *A* and the final one the rondo will modulate to other keys, as did the sonata.

These are just the barest outlines of the larger forms, but should be enough to help you recognize them. Remember, though, that these designs are just the most typical patterns; there is a great deal of variation in these forms and there are other patterns that have grown out of them. The ingenuity employed by composers in shaping large works is a subject that can be studied in great depth.

Summary, Chapter XII

1. The binary and ternary song forms are built from contrasting phrases or phrase groups, which in diagrams are represented as *A* and *B*. The *binary* song form can be represented as *AA'BB'*, where the accents mark a closed phrase ending. The *rounded binary* song substitutes a return of the *A* material in place of the second *B*, as in *AA'BA'*. The *ternary* song has three parts: *ABA*. These forms can be expanded: in a simple folk song each letter may refer to only a single phrase; in a larger composed song the letter may stand for a phrase group or a still larger section of music.

2. Other ways of organizing music include schemes of repeating chord progressions or repeating melodies. A piece built on a repeating chord progression can be called a *chaconne*. A *passacaglia* is based on a repeated melody that is usually in the bass but can appear in other voices. Such a repeated accompaniment melody is itself called an *ostinato*.

3. The word *canon* generally refers to a tune that is written so that it can provide its own accompaniment. One player begins the tune and after the first player has reached a certain point another one joins in, playing from the start. A *round* or *circular canon* is a special kind of canon whose ending harmonizes its beginning, so that it can be repeated endlessly.

4. Large pieces of music often have forms that are distant relatives of the basic song forms. Several important large forms are included in the classical *symphony*, a work for orchestra that is usually divided into four *movements* or sections.

5. The first movement of a classical symphony is almost always in *sonata form*, which resembles a greatly expanded rounded binary form. The typical sonata's form is based on harmony: the first half, the *exposition*, modulates to the dominant; the next half begins with a *development* section that starts in the dominant and may pass through other keys. The *recapitulation* is again in the tonic key and features material from the first section. The recapitulation corresponds to the return of *A* in rounded binary form.

6. The second movement of a symphony is usually a slow movement built on an expanded song form. In some cases it may be a *theme and variations*, in which you hear first a simple, usually well-known, melody and then many variations of it. The goal in such a movement is to vary the tune in interesting ways while still allowing it to be recognized.

7. The third movement is traditionally a *minuet and trio*, two dances based on rounded binary form. The minuet is usually the most vigorous and dance-like, with the trio having a contrasting lyrical character and a different key. After the trio the minuet is played again, so that the movement as a whole also has an *ABA* form.

8. The last movement of a symphony is frequently in *rondo* form, which follows the pattern *ABACAD...A*. A rondo is distinguished primarily by the repeated returns of the *A* material, called the *rondo theme*.

XIII. VOICE-LEADING

Though we have spoken in detail of individual chords and chord progressions, it is also useful to consider harmony not as a series of chords but as several lines of melody that form chords between them as they move. Generally the best results are obtained when each of those melodies is graceful in itself and cooperates well with the others without losing its independence. Musicians have evolved a number of effective techniques to attain these goals, which we study as the art of *voice-leading* or *counterpoint*.

In the following example four voices combine to form a series of chords. The voices are first written on separate staves so that you can easily see the melody of each one, and then they are combined on a single grand staff, as they probably would appear in sheet music. On almost every beat a new chord is formed by the combined voices. The music is from a chorale setting by J.S. Bach, *Herzlich lieb hab ich dich, o Herr.*

Figure 1. A Bach chorale in score and in piano reduction

The basic chords formed by the voices of that chorale are easier to recognize if the nonharmonic tones are removed:

Figure 2. Extracting chords from the chorale

You can see how the chords are formed from the movement of the four voices of melody. But, at the same time, each of the individual voices is a singable line that, especially with the added nonharmonic tones, follows the rules of melody writing discussed earlier.

Similarly, even keyboard music in the tonal style can be reduced to the underlying chords, though the movement of individual "voices" may not be so clear. However, what voices there are will often make singable lines. For example, if we simplify the broken chords in the bass clef of this Mozart piano sonata we see that they are essentially three-part harmony. Add the melody in the upper staff and we again have four melodic voices underlying the piece, and each makes a singable line.

Principles of Voice-Leading

Successful voice-leading in tonal music depends on three things: a good melody for each voice, sufficient independence for each voice, and resolution of any dissonances formed between the voices. Each of these will be treated in more detail below.

Figure 3. Underlying four-part harmony in a Mozart piano sonata

Economy of Motion

When making a chord change, try to voice the second chord in such a way as to minimize the amount of movement required by each voice. This produces smoother melodies within the harmony.

For example, if the new chord has notes in common with the preceding one, then perhaps those notes should be repeated in the same voice. Perhaps you can arrange things so that none of the voices needs to move more than a second in order to reach the notes of the new harmony, as in figure 4. The principle of *economy of motion*, which helps to achieve smooth and connected melodic lines, is one that is valid in modern jazz and pop as well as in the classical style.

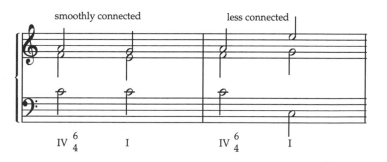

Figure 4. Voicing for economy of motion

Independence of Voices

The relative motion of a pair of voices can be *similar, parallel, contrary,* or *oblique*:

 Figure 5. Types of motion

similar   parallel   contrary   oblique

The types of motion that produce the greatest sense of independence are, of course, contrary and oblique motion, and then similar motion. Parallel motion is frequently used in harmony, but mostly using the weaker imperfect consonant intervals like the third and sixth, as in this example:

Land   of   the   pil-   grims'pride,   land   where   our   fa-   thers died,

Figure 6. Parallel motion of imperfect consonances

Parallel motion of the strong perfect intervals of the fifth or the octave is avoided in traditional writing for several parts because it seems to reduce the independence of voices: the parallel parts can give the impression of being one voice with a brassy tone quality. A composer attempting four-part polyphony would avoid the following (parallels are marked with heavy lines).

 Figure 7. Undesirable parallel perfect consonances

Fourths are perfect intervals, but they are not as strong as fifths and octaves and are treated differently. They are sometimes written in parallel if neither voice is the bass and if they are combined with thirds or sixths.

Avoidance of parallel perfect intervals is a matter of style—their sound is appropriate when produced by choice. But if you want to create a genuinely polyphonic texture then avoiding parallels is a valuable skill.

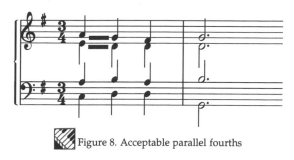

Figure 8. Acceptable parallel fourths

Resolving Dissonance

A composition would be a dull thing if it contained only consonant harmonies. Most pieces employ frequent dissonances. In the tonal harmony we are studying, however, close attention is paid to how dissonances are *approached* and how they are *resolved* to a consonance. For our purposes it will be enough to state just two basic principles for handling dissonances:

1) A dissonance should be resolved to a consonance before proceeding to another dissonance (don't write two dissonant notes in a row).

2) A dissonance is usually approached by step and almost always is resolved by step. Sometimes it can be approached by leap, if it is resolved by step in the opposite direction.

Most dissonances that you will encounter in tonal music are treated according to these principles. All of the dissonant notes in the Bach chorale of figure 9, for example, are approached by step and then immediately resolved by step. Here is that example again, this time with the dissonant notes circled (we have not marked *all* nonharmonic tones — just the dissonances):

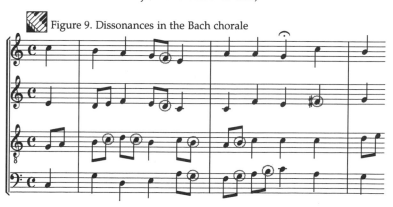

Figure 9. Dissonances in the Bach chorale

All but one of the dissonances occur in rhythmically weak (unaccented or offbeat) positions. Only one accented dissonance appears, the F# on the last beat of the second measure. The distinction between accented and unaccented dissonances is useful because you will need to be more strict in the treatment of accented dissonances. Unaccented dissonances will occasionally leap to a resolution but accented ones almost always resolve by step.

Nonharmonic Tones

The *nonharmonic* or *nonchordal tones* mentioned above and in chapter 10 can be classified into several common types, which are found in both classical and popular music. Knowing these typical nonharmonic tones will help you to handle dissonances gracefully when writing music in several parts. These classifications apply in general to any decorative tones that are not part of the current chord, dissonant or not, but they are essentially techniques for handling dissonance.

The Passing Tone

When a melodic line moving stepwise departs just briefly from consonance to "pass through" a dissonant interval we call the dissonant note a *passing tone*. These are usually unaccented but can be placed on the beat. In these examples the dissonant passing tones are circled, and the notes that follow them are the consonant notes that resolve the dissonance.

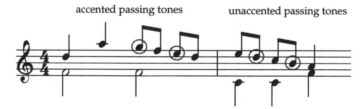

Figure 10. Passing tones

Passing tones are by far the most common type of dissonance. If you look again at the Bach chorale in figure 9, you'll see that every dissonance in it can be described as a passing tone, even the F♯ in the last chord of measure two.

The Neighboring Tone

The *neighboring tone* (also called the *auxiliary tone*) is like a passing tone, but it comes back to where it started instead of continuing up or down the scale, as follows:

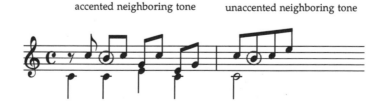

Figure 11. Neighboring tones

The Appoggiatura

The *appoggiatura* is an accented dissonance that is approached by leap and which then moves by step to a consonant interval. The leap is usually upwards and the resolution usually downwards:

Figure 12. The appoggiatura

Figure 13. The escape

The Escape

This relatively rare device is the opposite of an appoggiatura: the *escape* is unaccented, approaches by step, and resolves by leap.

The Suspension

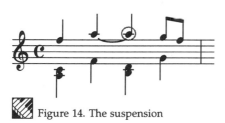
Figure 14. The suspension

In the *suspension* a harmonic tone is held or repeated to become a dissonance with the following chord change. Like the appoggiatura, the dissonance occurs on an accented beat and its resolution is usually downward by step. In figure 14 the tied note is a suspension; it becomes dissonant with the accompaniment on beat three. This suspension could just as easily have been written with a half note instead of the two tied quarters.

The Anticipation

The anticipation is a nonharmonic tone that anticipates a following change in the other voices. It is resolved when the other voices "catch up" with the anticipation tone:

Figure 15. The anticipation

The Pedal Point

Derived from the pedal of an organ, this term refers to any long sustained note that becomes dissonant as the other parts move. It is usually a bass note, but can be in other voices.

 Figure 16. The pedal point

Bach chorales are rich sources for illustrations of voice-leading practice. This one,
Herzlich thut mich verlangen, includes two sus-
pensions of the repeated-note type, which are in
the alto voice (the next-highest) on beat four of
the first measure and beat one of the second.

Figure 17. J.S. Bach: *Herzlich thut mich verlangen*

Figure 18. Avoiding parallel fifths

Notice in both chorale examples how Bach is careful to avoid parallel fifths or octaves. You can
examine his work by finding every fifth or octave in the harmony and then checking the relative motion
of the voices as they move to the following interval. The motion is almost always contrary or oblique,
as in the first two beats (figure 18).

Launch the Textbook Activity *13.1 Chorale Writing* for practice in writing four-part harmony. Though chorales are usually
seen notated on two staves, you'll be presented with a separate staff for each voice to make it easier to edit each part. For this
simple exercise we will not start with a melody but with several chords written out in four parts. Your task is to rewrite them
according to good voice-leading principles, using the following example as a model.

Writing in the Chorale Style

The starting chords in figure 19 are moving in parallel, and so the harmony is full of parallel fifths and octaves. It would be better if each of the parts had some degree of independence, which we can obtain by *revoicing* the chords (rearranging their notes).

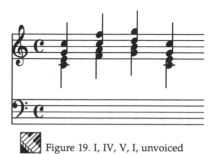

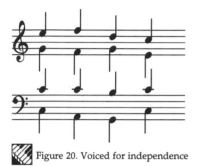

Figure 20. Voiced for independence

In figure 20 each voice now has a melody different from the others, and though the harmonies are exactly the same the composition is more interesting. You can see how chord inversions arise; we put the IV chord in first inversion to make a descending bass line on beat two. The other chords are still in root position, but they have been spread out into open voicing and the upper notes of each chord are in a different order. We've also avoided getting either very high or very low, since the traditional ideal for part-writing is the vocal quartet of soprano, alto, tenor, and bass.

Figure 19. I, IV, V, I, unvoiced

However, we've still used only the same notes that we started with, all of which form consonant harmonies. A few dissonances would add both interest and movement. In places where a voice leaps by a third we could insert passing tones, as in figure 21:

A suspension would add a little drama to the penultimate chord. The C in the tenor voice is one step above a chord tone for beat three; we'll tie it over onto the beat and resolve it downward to the chord tone (figure 22).

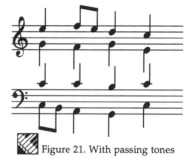

Figure 21. With passing tones

Figure 22. Adding a suspension

Simple as it is, this four measure composition is certainly a great advance over the plain chords of figure 19! And though it is written in a style modeled after that of Bach, the voice-leading principles involved are also found in other types of music.

The avoidance of parallel perfect intervals is mostly important for music that has a set number of voices, such as vocal music or music for several melody instruments. But even in classical piano music we can often see some evidence of the voice-leading principles, as in the below example from Mozart, the same sonata that was quoted in figure 3. The dissonances in these three measures are a little harder to recognize than those of the Bach because the Alberti bass breaks up the chords; in figure 23 the lower staff is a reduction of the harmonies in the Alberti bass.

Figure 23. The Mozart sonata with a reduction of the Alberti bass

Most of the dissonance in this excerpt is in measure two. The F in the first chord of measure two is an accented neighboring tone that resolves by downward step to an E in the second chord of that measure. The D beneath it could also be called an accented neighboring tone if we consider this fourth to be dissonant, as Mozart probably did (the fourth is usually considered dissonant if one of its notes is the bass). The C in the right hand (upper voice) is also a dissonance in that G major triad, but it is a passing tone that resolves by step to a consonant D. The F on the first beat of the third measure is another technically-dissonant fourth that resolves downward by step.

Though the music of Bach and Mozart seems most of the time to "follow the rules" of dissonance handling and voice leading that is not to say that either composer was restricted in any way. Both composers learned various rules as the means of writing what they wanted to write. Neither would have considered these rules to be an infringement of his freedom — the rules were, and are, just a way to achieve a desired result.

Summary, Chapter XIII

1. It is helpful sometimes to think of harmony not as a series of chords but rather as several simultaneous melodies.

2. Voice-leading is the art of making several melodies work gracefully together to make harmonic changes.

3. Successful voice-leading depends on a good melody for each voice, sufficient independence for each voice, and resolution of any dissonances formed between the voices.

4. Voice-leading benefits from *economy of motion*: when changing chords the movement between voices should be minimized. Each voice should, if possible, move to the nearest available tone of the next chord.

5. The relative motion of a pair of voices can be *parallel* or *similar*, *contrary*, or *oblique*. Parallel motion at the perfect fifth and octave should be avoided in the classical style.

6. Parallel fourths are less objectionable than parallel fifths if they do not involve the bass and are combined with thirds or sixths.

7. General rules for dissonances:

   (1) A dissonance should be resolved to a consonance before proceeding to another dissonance (don't write two dissonant notes in a row).

   (2) A dissonance is usually approached by step and almost always is resolved by step. Sometimes it can be approached by leap, if it is resolved by step in the opposite direction.

8. The nonharmonic or nonchordal tones are specific ways of treating dissonances. In rough order of their frequency they are the *passing tone*, the *neighboring tone*, the *suspension*, the *appoggiatura*, the *pedal point*, the *anticipation* and the *escape*.

XIV. EXPRESSION MARKS

Expression marks are used to provide extra information about the way a passage is to be played. These performance indications are "extras" — they don't have to be there but are often helpful. They are relatively new in music notation — composers before the late 18th century made sparing use of expressive marks, depending instead on the musicians' knowledge of prevailing style. Nonetheless, editors often add them to older pieces as suggestions for the performer.

Dynamics

Indications of loud and soft are easy to understand once you know that *forte* means loud and *piano* means soft. Just remember that our keyboard instrument called the "piano" got its name from being able to play both soft and loud (*piano* is short for *pianoforte*). *Forte* is abbreviated *f* and *piano* is abbreviated *p*.

All the other dynamic markings are built from these: *ff* (*fortissimo*, or very loud), *mf* (*mezzo-forte*, or moderately loud), *mp* (*mezzo-piano*, or moderately quiet), and *pp* (*pianissimo*, or very quiet). Sometimes you'll see further extremes like *fff* or *ppp*, but it doesn't make much sense to keep on adding *f*'s and *p*'s beyond three. Aaron Copland once wrote *ppppp* under a very high note in music for a flute, but perhaps he was just making a little joke (it's very difficult to play a high note quietly on a flute).

ppp   pp   p   mp   mf   f   ff   fff

Figure 1. Dynamic indications   quiet   loud

Crescendo and Decrescendo

A *crescendo* (a gradual increase in volume) can be indicated by either the abbreviation, "cresc." or by a wedge that expands to the right. *Decrescendo* is the opposite. You may also see the words *diminuendo* (diminishing) or *morendo* (dying away) used for a decrescendo.

 Figure 2. Crescendo and decrescendo

Signs Affecting Articulation

The *staccato* sign is a dot placed below the note head, or above it if the stem is downward. It tells the musician to play this note clearly separated from the next one. Often this is misinterpreted to mean that a staccato note should be as short as possible, but really it just means to put a little "air" between the notes—as if there were a rest between them. The amount of separation necessary depends on the tempo and mood of the music; ultimately it is a matter of taste. Staccato can even be put on notes of long value:

Could be interpreted this way:

Figure 3. Staccato

If you want to emphasize that certain notes are *very* short you should combine a shorter note value with the staccato sign, or use the *wedge*, which calls for an extra-short staccato.

Figure 4. Staccato dots and wedges

The opposite of staccato is *tenuto*, which just means "held out." The tenuto sign is a horizontal line, written in the same place as the staccato sign. Often it carries an additional meaning of a certain emphasis to be given the marked notes.

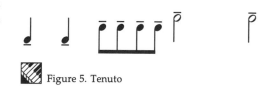
Figure 5. Tenuto

Accent

An accent mark is a short horizontal wedge over a note head, meaning that the note should be played forcefully (with a strong attack). Another way to indicate the same thing is the sign *sf*, which stands for *sforzando*, meaning "forced."

Figure 6. Accent marks

Slurs and Phrasing Marks

The *slur* looks like the *tie*, except that it connects two or more notes of different pitch. The effect is to make the notes *legato*, or smoothly joined together. A violinist will avoid lifting the bow between slurred notes; a singer or a performer on a wind instrument will do them in a continuous breath. On the piano, legato notes are joined by holding the first one until the next one begins.

A *phrase mark* looks like a very long slur, except that you aren't really expected to play all the notes within it slurred together: the mark only suggests that these notes should be thought of as part of the same musical idea. The end of a phrase is often marked by the "taking of a breath": a drop in loudness, a short rest, or even a very slight pause in the counting of time. Phrase marks cover more than a single measure, while most slurs connect just a few notes. If you see a phrase mark in a classical work from the time of Mozart and Beethoven it is probably an editorial suggestion — composers of that era generally left phrasing up to the performer. Even today performers will find their own ways of phrasing a piece unless the composer's intentions are unequivocal.

 Figure 7. Slurs and a phrase mark

Tempo Indications

The speed, or *tempo*, of a piece is traditionally indicated in Italian using such terms as *allegro* (fast), *andante* (walking), *adagio*, (slow) and so on. Many of these terms have colorings to their meaning that go beyond mere speed of execution, however. For example, *adagio* is not only slow but sad, whereas *maestoso* is slow but stately and positive. Sometimes a certain musical effect or figure is associated with a tempo indication: *maestoso* will often feature dotted rhythms implying a ceremonial procession, whereas *andante* often involves steady ("walking") eighth notes in the bass. *Allegro* is frequently not only fast but hopeful, positive, or even heroic, whereas *presto* is fast and just exciting, sometimes in a lighter mood.

Composers since the time of Beethoven often add a metronome mark as well, which is a precise measure of beats per minute. But the metronome mark lacks the emotional associations mentioned above. Metronome rates are measured as ticks per minute; a marking of ♩ = 50 means fifty quarter notes to the minute. Often the mark is labeled M.M. (Maelzel Metronome), after the inventor.

These are the most common of the tempo indications, from slowest to fastest:

largo , lento , adagio , andante, moderato, allegretto, allegro, presto

Common Italian Musical Terms

Accelerando. Accelerating.

Ad libitum. at will. Abbr. ad lib.

Andante. Walking speed.

Al fine. To the end.

Arco. With the bow (see *pizzicato*).

A piacere. Freely (with regard to rhythm).

Assai. Very.

A tempo. Return to previous tempo.

Brio. Brilliance.

Cantabile. Singing.

Con. with, e.g., *Allegro con brio.*

Crescendo. Getting louder.

Da capo. Repeat from the beginning. Abbr. D.C.

Dal segno. Repeat from the sign. Abbr. D.S.

Diminuendo. Diminishing.

Due. Two.

-issimo. Suffix meaning "very much", e.g., *fortissimo.*

Largo. Very slow.

Legato. Connected, smooth.

Lento. Slow.

L'istesso tempo. The same tempo.

Ma. but, e.g., *Allego ma non troppo.*

Maestoso. Majestically.

Marcato. Stressed.

Meno. Less, e.g., *meno mosso.*

Moderato. Moderately.

Molto. Very much, e.g., *Molto allegro.*

Mosso. Motion.

Non. Not.

Pizzicato. Plucked. Abbr. pizz.

Più. More.

Poco. A little.

Rallentando. Gradually slowing.

Ritardando. Slowing.

Secco. Dry.

Segue. Follows in the same way.

Sempre. Always.

Senza. Without.

Simile. Similarly.

Sostenuto. Sustained.

Sotto. Below, under.

Subito. Suddenly.

Tacet. Silence.

Tanto. Much.

Tre. Three.

Troppo. Too much.

Vivace. Lively.

Voce. Voice.

Summary, Chapter XIV

1. The expressive signs provide information that often would be provided by the interpretive skill of the performer. They are generally used only when a composer wants to ensure that the performer will play a passage in a certain way.

2. The *staccato* sign indicates that a note is to be clearly separated from the following note. This generally has the effect of making the note sound short. The sign for staccato is a dot placed above or below a note head, depending on the stem direction. The *wedge*, ▼, is also placed above or below the note head, and can be used to indicate an exaggerated staccato.

3. The *tenuto* sign, a short line placed above or below the note head, indicates that the note should be held out as long as possible (but without actually joining it to the next note).

4. The *accent mark*, >, means that a note is to be played with a strong attack.

5. Dynamics are indicated by the abbreviations of the Italian words *pianissimo, piano, mezzopiano, mezzoforte, forte, fortissimo*: *pp, p, mp, mf, f, ff.*

6. Gradually increasing loudness, or *crescendo*, is indicated by the word *cresc.* or by the sign, ——————. *Decrescendo, diminuendo*, and *morendo* are all words for decreasing loudness, as is the sign, ——————.

7. The *slur* looks like a tie except that it connects two or more notes of different pitch. Slurred notes are played smoothly joined together.

8. A *phrase mark* looks like a very long slur, longer than a measure; it shows the unity of a musical idea. It does not necessarily mean that all the notes under it are smoothly joined, just that they belong in one "breath."

9. *Tempo* is indicated usually just at the beginning of a piece, generally with an Italian word such as *allegro* (fast), *adagio* (slow), etc. Sometimes composers add the more precise metronome mark, such as ♩ = 60, which would mean 60 quarter notes to the minute.

10. Expressive indications are usually written in Italian, which has long been the international language for music notation.

APPENDICES

The Physics of Music

Partials

All sound is vibration, but the pitched sounds used in music are vibrations at a constant rate per second, called the *frequency of vibration*. For most people's ears the lowest frequency that sounds like a musical tone is about 27 vibrations per second, about that produced by the lowest note on a full-sized piano. The highest frequency we can hear diminishes as we grow older but at its best rarely exceeds 16,000 cycles per second, about two octaves above the highest note of a piano. The ability to hear high pitches (or, as we'll see below, the high components of lower notes) is permanently damaged by exposure to loud sounds, something that should be borne in mind when attending amplified concerts.

Since sound vibration amounts to a fluctuation in air pressure it is often represented in two-dimensional graphic form with time running on the horizontal axis and pressure on the vertical axis, as at right.

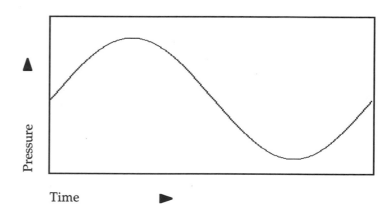

The graph shows a smooth increase and decrease in pressure which, if repeated 110 times a second, would sound like a very colorless "A" two octaves below middle C. This simple curve follows the shape of the mathematical sine function, and so it is called a *sine wave*. However, sounds created by acoustic (i.e., not electronic) musical instruments are never so plain as this, because any physical object is too complicated to produce only a sine wave when it vibrates. For example, here is the waveform of part of a note played by a trumpet:

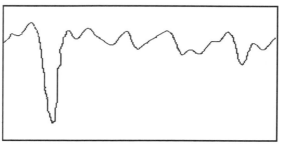

The trumpet waveform can be analyzed as the sum of many sine waves of different frequency, all of which are being heard simultaneously. That's why natural sounds are said to be *complex*; they are a mixture of many different frequencies, called *partials*.

In pitched sounds — sounds with a repeating waveform— the partials have an interesting relationship to each other which can be illustrated by examining a hypothetical vibrating string. If you pluck a string that is tightly stretched between two points it will vibrate along its whole length, creating a waveform like the sine wave above, but it will also vibrate in halves, thirds, fourths, fifths, etc. The figure below illustrates, in a very exaggerated way, the first three modes of vibration of a taut string:

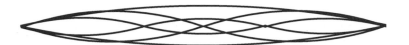

The various modes of vibration give rise to additional tones that complicate the wave form graph. Ideally (if the string is perfectly flexible and even) each of these other tones has a frequency closely related to the original one produced by the whole string. If the whole string is vibrating at 110 cycles per second, half of it will vibrate at twice 110, or 220; a third of it will vibrate at three times 110, and so on. Each of these other vibrations will sound like a pitch, so that the sound of the whole vibrating string is actually a combination of many partials. Partials having this relationship of 1,2,3...times the fundamental frequency are called *harmonic partials*, or *harmonics*, and if you listen very carefully to a vibrating guitar string, you can actually hear them. For example, if you played a low "A" you would hear the harmonics shown at right. Performers of stringed instruments sometimes isolate a particular harmonic by touching the string at one of the division points or *nodes*; this dampens all the partials that don't divide at that point and makes the harmonic easier to hear.

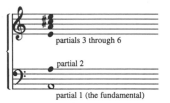

partials 3 through 6

partial 2

partial 1 (the fundamental)

Since the same phenomenon occurs with columns of air, as in the trumpet, and in fact any vibrating body, the harmonic series is part of all musical sounds. In some instruments, like bells, the partials are distorted by the stiffness of the material, but most pitched instruments make a fairly accurate harmonic series at least as high as we can hear it. This brings us to the importance of the harmonic series for harmony.

If you play two notes at the same time they will each have their own harmonic series, and if the two notes happen to have just the right relationship to each other some of those harmonics may match or come close to matching. For example, suppose you play A and E together. If the shared harmonics *almost* match, an interference pattern is created that sounds like a wavering or *beating*. You can, however, carefully raise or lower the pitch of one of the notes until the beating stops, which will happen when the coincident harmonics match exactly. At that point the two notes will seem to be in "agreement." We could also say that they are "in tune."

It is difficult to hear harmonics beyond the first six or so, since they become faint, but the first six are enough. The sixth is a convenient place to stop for other reasons as well: the seventh harmonic would create an interval that had no possibility of agreement with any of the first six, and the eighth harmonic is merely an octave, so the next practical one is the ninth, which is so quiet that it can't have much effect on the harmony. The first six harmonics give us all of the musical intervals that have the potential, if adjusted carefully, of being in agreement or being "consonant." In fact, our ear accepts these as being basically in agreement even if they are slightly out of tune; our tolerance seems to extend to the point where the beats become too fast to be easily counted. However, not all intervals have this potential for consonance, because not all of them have matches among the most easily-heard harmonics. The intervals with a clear potential for agreement are the unison, octave, fifth, fourth, major and minor thirds, and major and minor sixths. The other intervals, such as the second, have no possibility of matched harmonics among the first six, and so we regard them as being comparatively unrelated, unstable, or "dissonant."

If you are using one of Practica Musica's sampled instruments (i.e. anything but MIDI, QuickTime, or Synth) you can try this experiment: select Temperament from the Sound Options menu and choose the "Just" tuning. Now play the C major triad and listen very carefully, preferably with a set of headphones. The Just tuning allows you to hear the C major triad in its theoretically perfect form, with each note smoothly agreeing with the other. The effect is particularly noticeable with the organ. Contrast the sound of the justly-tuned triad with the same chord tuned to the Pythagorean system, which has a third that is considerably sharper than just. Once you can hear that distinction, compare the just C major triad to that of equal temperament, where the third is about halfway in sharpness between Pythagorean and Just.

Instrumental color

Different musical instruments give varying emphasis to each of the partials, which accounts for a large part of each instrument's characteristic "color." The clarinet, for example, emphasizes just the odd-numbered partials, whereas the oboe is rich in all of them. The highest partials of the piano are quieter than those of the harpsichord, and they are also more distorted, since the strings of the piano are thicker in relation to their length. The superior sound of a full-size grand piano is largely due to the longer and relatively thinner strings, which allow more accurate partials and clearer tone.

Changes in partials are also an important part of instrument color: plucked strings like those of the guitar begin with many partials and lose the higher ones as the sound dies away; a trumpet note, conversely, can begin with relatively few partials and gain more as it progresses.

Extraneous noises are significant for some instruments, though we may notice them only when they are missing. These include the wind or "chiff" at the beginning of a note played by a large organ pipe, the thunk of a piano hammer against the string, and the scraping sounds produced by a violin bow as it attempts to start a string moving. There are also various other tones that come from the resonance of other parts of the instrument: the tone of the various wood parts of a violin mixes with the tone produced by the bowed string, for example. The result is that the sound of an acoustic instrument can be extremely complex, which is why it is so difficult to imitate electronically.

Temperament

You would think that the ideal way to tune your piano would be to make each of the consonant intervals sound exactly in tune, so that no beating could be heard. Indeed, many musicians have long regarded this as a sort of ideal, but it doesn't work out very well on a keyboard with only twelve keys to the octave. For example, you can tune your A so that it will make a very nice sixth above your C, and the G as a good fifth above the C, and the D to make a good fifth below A, but then you'll find that the G will be out of tune with the D. In other words, it doesn't come out even; you can't tune all the consonances to be simultaneously exactly right unless you have two different keys for some of the notes, such as one D tuned to agree with G and another D made to work with A.

This problem was solved in many different ways over the years. The first solution was to tune the fifths exactly right and not to worry about the thirds and sixths, just as Pythagoras, the semi-legendary discoverer of musical mathematics, had done. This *Pythagorean* tuning was the basis of organ tuning and music theory until around the late 14th or early 15th century, which is why thirds and sixths were regarded before that time as dissonant intervals.

But when musicians began to want to use the consonant third a compromise had to be found, and they responded by tuning that troublesome D to the *mean* (average) of the two that were needed, which produced a system in which *most* of the thirds were very good and *most* of the fifths were only slightly off; this we now call *meantone temperament* (to "temper" an interval means to adjust its tuning a little bit away from perfect).

Meantone was used for several centuries and is still enjoyed by connoisseurs of early music, but it had one problem: since four of the less-common thirds were very discordant (and one fifth, the *wolf fifth*, was really awful), meantone didn't allow the free use of all the intervals in all the keys. So musicians began to alter the compromise a little with the hope of making the wolf and the bad thirds less objectionable. The *Vallotti* temperament is a variant of meantone in which the wolf is gone, the bad thirds are not quite so large, and the good thirds are, in trade, not quite so good as they were in normal meantone. Other people invented schemes in which some chords have both perfect thirds and perfect fifths and others have varying shades of inexactness; the *Kirnberger* temperament is an example. In these tunings that grew out of meantone there begins to be some variety in the quality of the acceptable chords, which may have contributed to the notion that different keys have different characters — for example, C major was thought to be pure and cheerful, while F# major was harsh and dark.

The temperament that won out in the end, at least so far, was *equal temperament*, in which all the thirds are just barely OK but all the fifths are very good. Equal temperament has much to recommend it; besides being the same in all keys its large major thirds are well-suited to melody, which is an important factor in our music. For some reason musicians often prefer large thirds for melody even though the smaller thirds make smoother harmony. Fortunately, most of us are able to accept the larger thirds in harmony, too, especially since the modern piano does not emphasize the higher overtones the way the harpsichord did. Nonetheless, many musicians experiment with tuning, and there may yet be something of a revival of alternate systems, even ones with more than 12 notes to the octave, which are much easier to implement with electronic musical instruments than they were with mechanical ones.

The following is a chart of each of the tunings and temperaments provided with *Practica Musica*. The variations in tuning are measured in *cents* (one cent = 1/1200 octave or 1/100 of an equal-tempered half step). The upper rows show the size of the major third above each note, as compared with the acoustically exact interval, and the lower rows show the same comparison for the fifth above the given note. A zero in either place means that the interval is acoustically exact and will sound without any "beating."

Equal temperament

14	14	14	14	14	14	14	14	14	14	14	14
F	C	G	D	A	E	B	F#	C#	G#	D#	A#
-2	-2	-2	-2	-2	-2	-2	-2	-2	-2	-2	-2

Pythagorean

22	22	22	-2	-2	-2	-2	22	22	22	22	22
F	C	G	D	A	E	B	Gb	Db	Ab	E	Bb
0	0	0	0	0	0	24	0	0	0	0	0

Meantone

0	0	0	0	0	0	42	42	42	42	0	0
F	C	G	D	A	E	B	F#	C#	G#	Eb	Bb
-5.5	-5.5	-5.5	-5.5	-5.5	-5.5	-5.5	-5.5	-5.5	37	-5.5	-5.5

Vallotti 1/6 comma

6	6	6	10	14	18	22	22	22	18	14	10
F	C	G	D	A	E	B	F#	C#	G#	Eb	Bb
-4	-4	-4	-4	-4	-4	0	0	0	0	0	0

Kirnberger 1/2 comma

11	0	0	0	9	20	20	20	22	22	22	22
F	C	G	D	A	E	B	F#	C#	G#	Eb	Bb
0	0	0	-11	-11	0	0	-2	0	0	0	0

Tempérament ordinaire

8.5	0	2.5	5	5.5	10	15	20	29	32	24.5	17
F	C	G	D	A	E	B	F#	C#	G#	Eb	Bb
3	-5.5	-5.5	-5.5	-5.5	-3	-3	-6	0	2	2	3

Just scale in C

0	0	0	0	22	22	20	20	20	20	22	22
F	C	G	D	A	E	B	F#	C#	G#	Eb	Bb
0	0	0	-22	0	0	0	0	0	-2	0	0

Extended meantone. Divides the octave into 35 notes without enharmonic equivalents, where every major third is exactly tuned and every perfect fifth is 5 1/2 cents flat.

Extended Pythagorean. Divides the octave into 35 notes without enharmonic equivalents, where every major third is 22 cents wide and every perfect fifth is exact.

Glossary

Aeolian mode. The mode or scale represented by the piano's white keys beginning with A. Equivalent to the modern *natural minor*.

accent.   1) An expression mark, $>$, that calls for emphasis on a note.

2) Metric accent: An accented note is one in a strong rhythmic position: on a beat or on a duple subdivision of a beat (such as the first or third of a group of four sixteenth notes).

accidental.   A sign used to raise or lower a note without changing its letter name. There are five accidental signs: ♮ ♯ ♭ 𝄪 𝄫

agogic. Pertaining to modification of tempo. An agogic accent brings a note into prominence through being slightly early or late.

alla breve. Duple meter in which the half note counts the beat; Cut time; 2/2.

anacrusis. Unaccented (upbeat) notes at the beginning of a phrase. The tune "The Itsy-Bitsy Spider" begins with an anacrusis (p. 15).

anticipation.   A nonharmonic tone that anticipates a following chord tone.

arpeggio.   A chord played one note after another, as on a harp.

asymmetrical meter.   A meter that is divisible by neither three nor two: e.g., 5/4, 7/8, etc.

augmented.   Enlarged one half step beyond major or perfect.

augmented sixth.   A sixth that is one half step larger than a major sixth.

augmented sixth chords.   Chords that include the augmented sixth built on the lowered sixth degree of the scale. The notes of the augmented sixth resolve in opposite directions to the dominant degree. Depending on what other notes are used in addition to the augmented sixth itself, the result will be either the "French," the "Italian," or the "German" augmented sixth chords, or one that is called the "doubly-augmented fourth."

augmentation. Variation by increasing the note values, as in rhythmic augmentation.

authentic cadence. A harmonic cadence of the chords V-I. See **plagal cadence.**

bass.   The lowest note in a chord or interval.

bass clef. The F clef, 𝄢, when placed so that it marks the first line down in a staff. See **clef, treble clef, C clef.**

beam.   A slanted or horizontal bar that connects two or more note stems as a replacement for the *flag.*

beat.   The steady pulse that underlies measured music.

cadence. A melodic or harmonic close to a musical phrase. See **authentic cadence, plagal cadence, half cadence.**

C clef. A clef, 𝄡, that marks the position of middle C. Most commonly found in the *alto* or *tenor* positions (middle line or 4th line up).

chord.   Any simultaneous combination of more than two pitch classes.

chromatic.   See **genera.**

chromatic half step. A half step in which the letter name does not change, e.g. C-C♯ . See **diatonic half step.**

clef. Symbol drawn in a staff to identify the pitches represented by each line or space. See **treble clef, bass clef, C clef.**

conjunct.   A melody with mostly stepwise motion is conjunct. See **disjunct.**

consonance.   An interval or chord is generally said to be consonant if its notes share one or more of the more easily heard overtones (the lower overtones are the easiest to hear). The shared overtones lend a sense of stability to the combination. The consonances in order of stability are the unison, octave, fifth, fourth (which, however, is considered dissonant under some circumstances— see **dissonance**), major third, minor third, major sixth, and minor sixth. "Consonance" is a relative term, as is "dissonance."

common time. A name for 4/4 meter.

compound meter. A meter in which the beat is represented by a dotted note; e.g. 3/8, 6/8, 9/8, 12/8. See **simple meter.**

crescendo. Getting louder gradually.

da capo . Italian "from the beginning." Abbr. "D.C."

da capo al fine . Italian "from the beginning to the marked *fine* (end)." Abbr. "D.C. al fine"

dal segno al fine . Italian "from the sign to the marked *fine* (end)." Abbr. "D.S. al fine."

decrescendo. Getting quieter.

diatonic. See **genera.**

diatonic half step. A half step in which the letter name changes, e.g. D-E♭.

diminished. Reduced; an interval one half step smaller than minor or perfect; a chord containing a diminished fifth and a minor third.

diminution. Variation by reducing note values, as in rhythmic diminution.

disjunct. A melody that moves largely by leaps is disjunct. See **conjunct.**

dissonance . An interval that is not acoustically stable, or which is treated as such in traditional music theory. Dissonant intervals are the seconds, sevenths, all augmented or diminished intervals, and the fourth when alone or involving the bass. See **consonance.**

dominant. The fifth degree of the scale, or the chord built on the fifth degree of the scale.

dominant seventh . A major chord with a minor seventh. In a major key it occurs naturally only on the fifth, or dominant, degree of the scale — hence the name.

Dorian. The church mode beginning on D, same pattern as the white keys starting on D.

dotted note. A note followed by a dot, which increases the note value by half and therefore makes the note a triple quantity rather than a duple one. Example: a dotted quarter note equals three eighth notes.

double-flat. The sign,♭♭,which lowers a note by two half steps.

double-sharp. The sign, ✕, which raises a note by two half steps.

doubling. Repeating one of the pitch classes in a chord.

downbeat. The first beat of a measure, which receives the strongest metric accent.

duple. Capable of being divided evenly by two.

dynamics. Loudness or softness.

enharmonic. Two notes, intervals, or chords are enharmonic with each other if they are spelled differently but sound the same on the piano. Examples: F♯ and G♭, major third and diminished fourth, German augmented sixth chord and dominant seventh chord. See **genera.**

escape. A nonharmonic tone approached by step and resolved by leap.

figured bass. (thoroughbass) The practice of writing numbers under the bass notes to indicate harmonies.

first inversion. A chord is in first inversion if its third is in the bass position.

flag. On a note stem, one of the rightward flaglike extensions used for notes shorter than a quarter note. See **beam.**

flat. The sign, ♭, which lowers a note one half step.

genera.   The ancient Greek genera were three ways of building a four-note scale within the space of a fourth. The *diatonic* genus broke the fourth up into two whole steps (tones) and a half step. A more unusual division was the *chromatic*, which consisted of two half steps of different size and a minor third. The last and most exotic was the *enharmonic*: a major third, a half step, and a tiny interval (smaller than a half step), called a *diesis*. All these words continue to have meanings based on their original significance to the Greeks. *Diatonic* music is music based on major or minor scales or the church modes; all of which are called diatonic because they resemble the diatonic genus above — they employ whole tones and that type of half step in which the note name changes. *Chromatic* music involves at least some half steps in which the note name remains the same, as in the chromatic genus. Similarly, the word *enharmonic* still refers to the relationship between two notes that are written differently and would in theory be separated by a *diesis*, and yet are played on the same key of the piano, such as E♯ and F. Below is an attempt to represent the genera in modern notation:

diatonic   chromatic   enharmonic

grand staff. The combination of treble clef and bass clef staves.

ground bass. An ostinato bass; a short bass melody that repeats as other parts vary.

half cadence. A cadence to the dominant chord or the subdominant chord; an unfinished cadence. See **authentic cadence.**

half-diminished.   Describes the type of seventh chord in which the fifth is diminished but the seventh is not. Ex.: BDFA

half step. Half of a whole step. The smallest step possible on a piano, e.g. E-F.

hemiola.   A special type of syncopation in which a duple pair is played in the time of a triple group, or vice-versa. Example: a pair of dotted eighth-notes in 3/8 meter.

interval.   The difference in pitch between two notes; the combination of the two.

intonation.   The degree of precision in pitch. The violin and the voice are examples of instruments capable of *free intonation*, because they can adjust the pitch in increments smaller than a half step.   Keyboard instruments have *fixed intonation.*

inversion.   An interval or chord can be inverted, exchanging the relative positions of its notes. C-E is the inversion of E-C.

Ionian.   The church mode beginning on C. Equivalent to the modern major scale.

key.   1) The scale being used, as in the *key* of D. 2) One of the claves, or levers, of the keyboard.

key signature.   At the beginning of each staff, the flats or sharps needed for the key are arranged in a key signature.

leading tone.   1) The seventh scale degree in a major, harmonic minor, or melodic minor scale 2) Any note that is a half step away from its apparent destination.

ledger line (leger line). A short line that extends the range of a staff upward or downward.

Lydian.   The church mode beginning on F; same pattern as the white keys starting on F.

major.   1) The larger of the two forms of the second, seventh, third, or sixth.
2) Also used to describe a scale or chord whose first third is major.

measure. A group of beats with the first one accented. Measures are separated by vertical *measure lines* through the staff.

mediant. The third note of a scale or the chord built on it.

meter. The beat-grouping of a piece: 3/4, 4/4, etc.

minor. 1) The smaller of the two forms of the second, seventh, third, or sixth. 2) Also used to describe a scale or chord whose first third is minor.

Mixolydian. The church mode beginning on G; same pattern as the white keys starting on G.

mode. Essentially equivalent to *scale*. Commonly used to refer to the church modes *Dorian, Phrygian, Lydian,* and *Mixolydian,* or any diatonic scales other than standard major and minor.

modulation. Moving to a different key within a composition.

natural. 1) Unaltered and played on the white keys of the piano.
2) The accidental sign, ♮, used to naturalize a note.

natural minor. The type of minor scale formed by the white keys starting on A.

neighboring tone (auxiliary tone) A nonharmonic tone approached by step and resolved stepwise in the opposite direction.

nonchordal tone. See **nonharmonic tone**.

nonharmonic tone. A dissonant tone or one not in the prevailing chord, such as a passing tone or a neighboring tone.

octatonic scale. An eight-tone scale that consists of alternating half steps and whole steps. It is not a traditional scale, but was used by some 19th-century Russian composers and by Igor Stravinski.

octave. The interval between any note and the next one bearing the same name, that is, having the same pitch class; e.g., C to C. C to C♯ would be an *augmented* octave; C to C♭ a *diminished* octave.

overtone. Also called a *partial*. Any musical tone is actually a complex of many *partials* in which the frequency of the most audible partials is approximately an integer multiple of the starting, or *fundamental*, frequency.

passing tone. A nonharmonic tone approached by step and resolved by step in the same direction.

pedal point. A long held tone that becomes nonharmonic as other notes change.

pentatonic. Composed of five tones. A pentatonic scale.

perfect. Describes a unison, octave, fifth, or fourth that is neither diminished nor augmented.

Phrygian. The church mode beginning on E; same pattern as the white keys starting on E.

pitch. The perceived "highness" or "lowness" of a note.

pitch class. Two notes have the same "pitch class" if their name is exactly the same (i.e., they are separated by one or more perfect octaves).

plagal cadence. A harmonic cadence of the chords IV-I. See **authentic cadence**.

primary triads. In any key, the chords built on the tonic, dominant, and subdominant degrees.

Pythagorean. Following the principles of Pythagoras, the semi-legendary Greek founder of the science of harmony. Specifically refers to a scale tuning in which all notes are derived by tuning a series of acoustically exact fifths.

resolve, resolution. A dissonant interval or chord generally resolves to a consonant one in classical tonal music, dissipating what is meant to be perceived as the tension of the dissonance.

root position. A chord is in root position if its root is also its bass.

scale. Any pattern of steps that fills in the space of an octave and which may be regarded as raw material for a piece of music. Scales were actually invented by theorists, who derived them from existing melodies.

second inversion. A chord is in second inversion if its fifth is in the bass.

semitone. A half step. Half of a whole tone.

sequence. The technique of developing a melodic fragment by repeating it in transposition, usually at the second.

sharp. A sign, ♯, used to raise a note by one half step.

simple meter. Meter in which the beat is counted by an undotted note, e.g. 2/2, 2/4, 4/4, 3/4. See **compound meter.**

solmization. The use of the syllables "do, re, mi..." to remember the sound of the major or minor scales; *solfège.*

staff. The five horizontal lines on which notes are written in *staff notation.*

subdominant. The fourth scale degree, or a chord built on that degree.

submediant. The sixth scale degree, or a chord built on it.

subtonic. The seventh scale degree. Usually called this only if it is a whole step away from the tonic. If it is just a half step from the tonic the seventh degree is called the *leading tone.*

supertonic. The second scale degree, or a chord built on it.

syncopation. In rhythm, a pattern that emphasizes the off-beats, usually by beginning notes on an offbeat and holding them over through the start of a beat.

temperament. If intervals are tuned acoustically exact they don't come out "even" with only twelve keys on the keyboard. Temperament systems make various compromises with acoustical exactitude for the sake of practicality. Equal temperament is the modern standard, in which all the major thirds are somewhat wide of their acoustically exact size and all the fifths are very slightly narrow.

tessitura. The range of pitches, particularly in vocal music. Popular songs tend to have a *tessitura* of little more than an octave.

tie. A curved line joining two adjacent notes of the same pitch to indicate that they sound as one.

tonal. Tonal music is based on the notes of a single diatonic scale, in which the tonic has the most important role. Both classical and popular music are tonal.

tonic. The first note of a diatonic scale.

transpose. To raise or lower the pitch of a passage, as in transposing a song from C major to D major.

treble clef. The G clef, 𝄞, when placed so that it circles the second line up in a staff. See **clef, bass clef, C clef.**

triad. A group of three notes, the pitch classes of which are separated by thirds, such as C,E,G.

triple. Capable of being divided evenly by three.

triplet. Rhythmically, three in the time of two.

tritone. The augmented fourth, which is equivalent to three whole tones.

unison. The interval composed of two notes having the same letter name and written on the same line or space. May be perfect, augmented, or diminished.

voicing. The spacing, doubling, and arrangement of the notes of a chord. Voicing may be altered without changing the harmony.

whole note. The basic unit of rhythm in notation. Equal to 4 quarter notes, 8 eighth notes, etc.

whole step, whole tone. An interval, such as C to D, equal to two half steps or semitones.

Music for Class Use

Rhythm Band

This is a kind of organized improvisation. Each person begins by playing the four-measure starting pattern, and then chooses one of the alternate measures and plays it at least four times. The player can continue to play the same measure, or can switch to a different one, but any chosen measure must be played at least four times before changing.

Players or groups enter in series: player 2 begins when player 1 has played the first four measures; player 3 enters when player 2 has finished those four measures, and so on to as many players as you like.

The staves used here are percussion staves, so each line refers not to a specific pitch but to a different percussive sound. Most of the patterns use two different sounds, so the note heads are on two different lines. For the best effect players should use two contrasting sounds and follow the pattern made by the note heads. "Instruments" can be anything that makes a sound, from clapping or tapping a pencil, to vocal sounds.

Starting pattern:

Alternates:
Choose any one and repeat at least 4 times. Then choose another or else continue with the same one.

Vocal Tuning

A. The Fat Chord: As a warm-up, and for fun, let each person begin singing *do*, all together, just one long note. When you run out breath, start again. After the *do* gets well started, let each person change at random to *mi* or *sol*, forming a triad. After a bit longer, try adding more notes to the mix, such as *la* or *re* or *fa* or *ti* (*si*). The only rule is this: hold the same note for as long as you can, singing lightly and gently. It's fun to build up a thick sound whose nature changes moment by moment as different people decide to try a different note. Listen carefully as you sing, and try to be "in tune" with the others. Stop when it seems right!

B. This is preparation for real part-singing. The class can divide into three groups, with the higher voices singing either of the upper parts. Each singer should listen carefully to everyone else, thinking hard about pitch. You may notice a tendency to sing the syllables *mi* and *la* slightly lower in pitch than the same pitches on a piano, which will sound good in this context.

It would be helpful for one person to conduct the others, using the conducting pattern for 4/4 described on page 22. If you want to practice outside class, open the Textbook Activity titled *Class Music* and follow the instructions for tapping your part.

Rounds

Divide the class into groups, as many groups as there are parts in the round. Group one starts first; group two enters when group one reaches the ✳. Group three enters when group two reaches the ✳, and so on. It will help if each student first learns the music using Practica Musica's Textbook Activity titled *Class Music*, where the complete scores for each of these can be found (Practica Musica will play the other parts as you tap the rhythm of one of them).

The music below is beamed in the vocal style: beams do not appear unless the beamed notes are sung on the same syllable.

Round 1, three parts: *The Great Bells of Oesney* (source: *Deuteromelia*, 17th c.)

Round 2, three parts: *John Cooke, You Be a Knave* (source: *Deuteromelia*, 17th c.)
Only the initials of the first words appear in the original: ICVBAK

Round 3, three parts: *Hey, Ho, Nobody Home* (source: *Deuteromelia*, with some alteration)

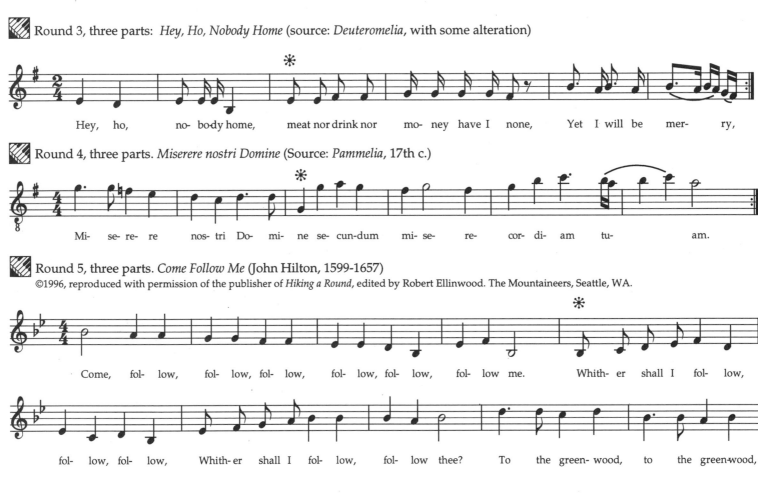

Hey, ho, no- bo-dy home, meat nor drink nor mo- ney have I none, Yet I will be mer- ry,

Round 4, three parts. *Miserere nostri Domine* (Source: *Pammelia*, 17th c.)

Mi- se- re- re nos- tri Do- mi- ne se- cun-dum mi- se- re- cor- di- am tu- am.

Round 5, three parts. *Come Follow Me* (John Hilton, 1599-1657)
©1996, reproduced with permission of the publisher of *Hiking a Round*, edited by Robert Ellinwood. The Mountaineers, Seattle, WA.

Come, fol- low, fol- low, fol- low, fol- low, fol- low, fol- low me. Whith- er shall I fol- low,

fol- low, fol- low, Whith- er shall I fol- low, fol- low thee? To the green- wood, to the green-wood,

to the green- wood, fol- low me!

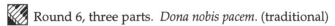 Round 6, three parts. *Dona nobis pacem.* (traditional)

Do- na no- bis pa- cem, pa- cem, do- na no- bis

pa- cem. Do- na no- bis pa- cem, do- na no- bis pa-

cem. Do- na no- bis pa- cem, do- na no- bis pa- cem.

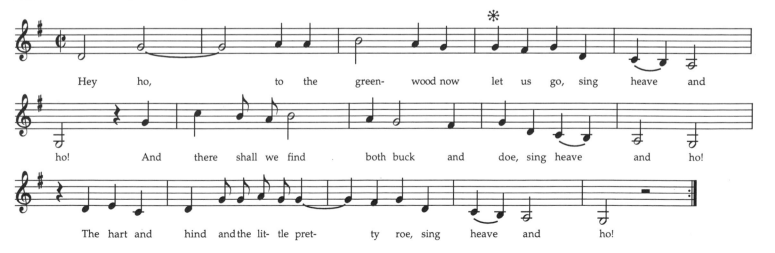 Round 7, three parts. *Hey, Ho, to the Greenwood.* Source: *Pammelia*, 17th c.

Hey ho, to the green- wood now let us go, sing heave and

ho! And there shall we find both buck and doe, sing heave and ho!

The hart and hind and the lit- tle pret- ty roe, sing heave and ho!

Round 8, five parts. *Let's Drink and Let's Sing* (William Hayes, 1757).

Note that each part begins with rests: don't skip over them!

Using *Practica Musica 4*

Getting Started

We will assume that you already know how to use your computer: how to handle a mouse, open folders, etc.. The following is information that is specific to Practica Musica. There is one basic instruction, however, applicable to everyone: experiment! If you are curious about a button or a menu item, choose it and see what happens. This is why children learn computing so quickly: they click on this and that until something works.

Installing Practica Musica

The Practica Musica CD can be read by either Macintosh or Windows computers. It requires at least Win 95/98 or Macintosh OS 7/8 or greater. The installer is self-explanatory and will place all the needed materials on your computer. If the installer does not automatically begin when you put the CD in the drive, double-click the CD icon named "Install Practica Musica" or "Practica Musica Setup."

When Starting the Program

• If you are using a floppy "Student Disk," place it in the disk drive before launching Practica Musica. If you are using the Student Edition CD, put the CD in the drive before launching Practica Musica.

• The first time you use the program, you'll be asked to provide your name, and in some cases your serial number, which is either on your Student Disk or on the disk sleeve of your CD. After the first time you sign in, a file with your name on it will appear in the Practica Musica Students folder. If there are a number of different students using Practica Musica you'll be asked to choose your personal file when you launch the program.

• In addition to the usual ways of launching a program, you can also launch Practica Musica by double-clicking on your Student File (the file in the Practica Musica Students folder that has your name on it) or on a Practica Musica Activity file.

Passwords

• If you are using Practica Musica in a shared environment you will want to enter a password for your Student File so that no one else comes along and changes your scores. Be sure to write down your password! There is no way to remove it without starting over from the beginning. If you didn't enter a password when you first signed in, there's an option in the File menu to add one later.

Setting up Sound

For efficient use of memory and speed in calculating sounds, we recommend that you use Practica Musica's QuickTime instrument (Macintosh), the Synth instrument (Windows) or MIDI (either platform). Practica Musica also includes sampled sounds, which can handle a great number of simultaneous voices but which need more time to prepare when you want to hear a passage. The sampled sounds are represented in the instrument list by pictures of various instruments, such as guitar, organ, etc.

MIDI input is always enabled in Practica Musica, regardless of your choice of output instrument.

• Macintosh: The QT/MIDI instrument is used for both the internal QuickTime synthesized instruments (the default setting) or for MIDI. If you intend to use MIDI input or output you'll need to change your default QuickTime settings. This needs to be done only once. Open the QuickTime Settings control panel (control panels are under the Apple Menu)and choose your input and output devices. This works best if you have at least QuickTime 3 or 4, available at no charge from Apple (for a link to Apple's QuickTime, see www.ars-nova.com).

• Windows: The program will use your default MIDI ouput devices and synthesizer card, and you can also choose specific devices in the Options menu.

• Both platforms: If using the sampled sounds (that is, anything but MIDI, QuickTime, or Synth) no configuration is needed.

Additional Activities

Ars Nova's *Activity Central* can be found at www.ars-nova.com. Here you can download the latest versions of activities and new activities as they are created. The same activity files will run on either Windows or Macintosh computers as long as the computer is equipped with Practica Musica 4 . Updates to Practica Musica 4 itself are here too, whenever they are available.

Because anyone with the standard or site edition of Practica Musica 4 can alter existing activities or create new ones, we cannot be sure of the contents of activities that don't carry the Ars Nova label. Activities created at Ars Nova will all have an Instructions menu item, and the Ars Nova logo will be visible in the Instructions window. We invite instructors to alter the standard activities or to create new ones, and we will be glad to post customized activities at Activity Central, filed under the name of the professor teaching the course.

Personal Scores

Your personal progress report is kept in your student file, a file bearing your name in the Practica Musica Students folder, and on your Student Disk if you have one. Your student file can easily be emailed to a teacher; simply send an email message and "attach" the student file. This works for both Macintosh and Windows; the file format is the same in both cases.

Personal Music

If you have produced any music files using Practica Musica, they can be emailed the same way as your student file. Anyone with either a Macintosh or a Windows computer and a copy of Practica Musica 4 or Songworks II or the free Songworks II Player (see www.ars-nova.com) can see and hear your music files.

Getting Help

If the following pages don't answer your questions, try reading the Frequently Asked Questions pages at www.ars-nova.com. This page will be updated as needed. Here you will also find descriptions of the latest activities and how to use them, though we hope that most activities will be self-explanatory.

The Activities Menu

The Activities menu displays all activities contained in the currently chosen activities folder, which can be any folder on your computer or on a connected server. If the desired activity is not displayed in the Activities menu, use the Change Activity Folder... command (in the Activities Menu) to find and open the activity you want. When you do, the Activities Menu will display the activities in the new folder.

Textbook Activities are located in a folder titled Textbook Activities, which is normally kept in the Activities folder (though you could put it anywhere). The folders are just to help you keep activities organized; you can add or remove activities from any folder, and you can create additional folders, if you like.

Choose any activity from the Activities menu and it will guide you with further instructions as it runs. Activities provided by Ars Nova also have an Instructions menu item that gives you brief directions.

The Active Staff

Each staff in the music window has a round handle at its left that you can drag with the mouse to move the staff. The active staff is the one that is currently selected to receive keyboard input (either external or from the screen piano or letter keys). You can identify the active staff by its solid red handle.

Most activities use either a single staff or the grand staff displayed as a single unit with one staff handle. The single staff and the grand staff are always active and ready to receive keyboard input.

In the case of an activity with two or more separate staves only the active staff will receive keyboard input. You can activate a different staff by clicking on any symbol in the staff or by clicking on its handle.

Playing Notes

You can use any of these methods for playing notes:

• Click on the keys of the screen piano using the arrow tool.
• Use the letter keys of the computer as a piano (see below).
• Play notes through an external MIDI keyboard.

If the cursor is shaped like a musical symbol that symbol will be entered in the staff when you play a note! If you only want to play notes without entering anything, choose the arrow tool.

The Letter Keys "Piano"

A MIDI keyboard is not required for most Practica Musica activities. If you don't have a MIDI keyboard connected to your computer, the letter keys can serve as a substitute "piano." The middle row of letters starting on "A" corresponds to the piano's white keys starting on C; the row above that contains the black keys. The lower row is not used for notes, but the "<" and ">" keys in the bottom row will lower and raise the pitch of the letter keys piano and the screen piano by octaves. Ars Nova sells a plastic piano overlay (*MiniKeys*)that can be set on top of the letters to make them more like a piano, but you can get along without it once you get used to the note positions. Just remember that the letters "F" and "G" play the notes F and G, but those are the only letters that correspond to their musical counterparts. If using QuickTime or MIDI, or the Windows Synth instrument you can even play chords on the letter keys piano.

Harmony Keys/Melody keys

The "Harmony Keys" and "Melody Keys" controls, when present, are found at the bottom left of the screen piano (see legend). Harmony Keys is used in some activities as the default setting to make it easier to play chords with the mouse. When harmony keys is "on" each note that you play stays highlighted on the piano and visible in the staff. It will turn off if you play it again, or if you use the spacebar to clear all current notes. With some activities you'll want to use Melody Keys instead, so that notes turn off with each key release. However, when using melody keys in an activity such as Chord Playing you will need to hold down the notes of the chord as you press "My answer is ready" so that the program can see which notes you intend as your answer.

Entering Notes on the Staff

In many cases an activity will select a note value for you so that all you are expected to do is to play a note in any of the ways described above. In other cases you may need to write notes on a staff using normal editing methods, as follows:

• You can enter notes directly on the staff by selecting a note value with the arrow tool and clicking in the staff where you want the symbol to appear.

• You can enter notes *at the current insertion point in the staff* (the blinking cursor) by selecting a note value and then playing the pitch as usual via the letter keys, or MIDI, or by clicking on the screen piano.

When you have selected a note or other symbol the cursor will be shaped like that symbol and will be entered in the staff when you play a note. If the cursor is an arrow, notes will play but nothing will be entered in the staff.

Entering Notes with Accidentals

To specify a flat, sharp, or other accidental select a note value and then click on the desired accidental box before entering the note in the staff. Selecting one of these will also work to force a black key to play as a flat or a sharp, if you are entering notes via the keyboard (or you can hold down the option key when playing the note to force a flat, or the command key to force a sharp).

Editing and Deleting Notes or Other Staff Symbols

As with a word processor, you can use the Delete/Backspace key to delete the symbol that precedes the current blinking insertion point. Most editing operations, however, require that a symbol or symbols be selected before any change can be made. For example, the Beam button works only on selected notes. Delete/Backspace will also delete any selected items, and selected items are the ones that will be copied if you use the Copy command, or Cut if you use Cut.

Items are selected for editing or deletion by clicking on them with the arrow tool. You can select a group of items by dragging a selection rectangle around the items using the arrow tool; click in the music, hold down the mouse button and drag. (Drag-select works only on items of the active staff.) Another way to select a large group of items in the active staff is to click on one side of the group (left or right), then hold down the Shift key and click on the other side. You can select several separate items by holding down the Shift key as you select the additional item (this is a standard way to select several items that are not adjacent). Deselect selected items by clicking anywhere else in the music.

Changing the Pitch of a Selected Note or Notes

To change the pitch of a note you've already entered, simply use the arrow tool to drag the note to the desired position on its staff. If you want to add a sharp or a flat to an existing note, select the note with the arrow tool and then click the sharp or flat button. Holding down the Option key as you sharp or flat a note will cause it to be a "precautionary" accidental, that is, it will be printed even if it's already in the key signature.

If you prefer to alter pitches via the keyboard or midi device, you can select the notes to alter, hold down the shift key, and play the desired pitches. In that case you can specify a sharp by holding down the Command (Mac) or Ctrl key (Win), and a flat by adding the Option (Mac) or Alt key (Win) as you play the note.

Changing the Rhythmic Value of a Selected Note or Notes

Change the rhythmic value of a selected note or notes by choosing the desired note value from the note tools above the screen piano (note tools do not appear in all activities).

Changing Other Symbols

In the same way, you can change any selected symbol to one of the same type (a clef to a different clef, or a meter to a different meter, or a rest to a different rest) by choosing the replacement symbol from one of the tool boxes above the screen piano.

Entering Text

• There are no activities that require you to enter text, but if you want to enter text in a composition activity, select the text tool, A , click in the music where you want the text to go, and start typing. Once entered, the text block can be selected and dragged with the arrow tool. It can also be copied and pasted as if it were a single symbol.

• Text sitting on a Lyric Line (one of the green lines that appears when you choose the Text Tool) will follow the spacing of the notes. When entering lyric text, click on a lyric line just slightly to the right of the note where you want the text to begin. Type the text, separating syllables with a hyphen or a space, but *don't add extra spaces to make the words line up with the notes!* When you're finished entering text, deselect the text tool and Practica Musica will line up the text automatically. If you later adjust the spacing of the notes, the text will follow automatically.

Hints for Activities

The following is not meant to provide instructions for every individual activity. We expect that more of them will be created each year. We have instead grouped together activities from the current set that fall into several basic types.

Real-time activities

In "real-time" activities you don't have to choose specific note values. Just listen carefully to the metronome and tap the desired rhythm using the middle row of letter keys or a MIDI keyboard (the mouse is not recommended for this). If the activity involves rhythm only, the letter keys piano works as well as a MIDI keyboard. Pick any two letter keys of the middle row, and alternate fingers as you tap. Use a light touch, keeping your fingers close to the keyboard; don't waste time raising them high between notes. With this technique you can play a complicated rhythm using nothing more than the computer keys and two fingers.

If the activity involves both rhythm and pitch it's best to use a MIDI keyboard for input.

Examples of rhythm-only real-time activities:

2.1. Beginning Rhythm	*Rhythm Reading*	*Active Listening*
4.1. Reading Syncopation	*Rhythm Matching*	*2-part Rhythm Reading*
12.1. Class Music		

Examples of pitch-and-rhythm real-time activities: *Pitch/Rhythm Reading*

Activities in which you enter pitches only

In these activities the rhythm values are automatically supplied. Only one note tool is supplied, if any, and the correct rhythm value is either automatic or not relevant. To enter a note, select the note tool if one is present, and either click in the staff or play the desired pitch or pitches on the piano. In activities where you must specify the flat or sharp, it may be easier to click in the staff instead of on the piano, unless the piano is the "enharmonic keyboard" (see the Options menu under Keyboard).

Examples of pitch-only activities:

10.1 Shaping Melody	*Pitch Matching*	*Progressive Pitch Dictation*
11.1 Tonal Sequencing	*Pitch Reading*	*Interval Playing*
Interval Spelling	*Chord Playing*	*Chord Spelling*

Activities in which you enter rhythm values only

Here you must choose specific note and rest values from those listed above the screen piano. Use the arrow tool to select and then click in the appropriate place on the staff. Pitches are supplied automatically.

Examples of rhythm-only activities:

3.2 Writing Rhythms   *Rhythm Dictation*

Activities in which you write on two or more staves

Here you need to remember the information from the discussion of the Active Staff, above. Only one staff is active at a time. Other than that, note entry and editing are the same as with one staff.

Examples of activities requiring writing on multiple staves:

3.1 Chorale Writing   *Two-Part Pitch Dictation*
Two and Four-Part Composition

Listening to Music Examples

Textbook music examples are listed by chapter and example number in the Textbook Activities folder. To listen, select the example and use Command-H or press the Listen button on the screen keyboard.

Changing tempo

You may wish to play the example faster or slower. Use Command-T or press the Tempo button to change the tempo (a higher number means a faster tempo).

The Metronome

The metronome icon is on the left side of the screen piano, above the sound on/off switch (see keyboard legend). Listening with the metronome turned on is often helpful when studying the rhythm of an example. In the Tempo window you'll also find the option of having the metronome play with a divided beat.

Play From and Play To controls

These controls are useful not only for textbook examples, but especially for dictation activities, because they let you hear just part of the example. Look for the two speaker-like controls at the top left of the music window (they are not present in every activity). Click on the left control—the cursor will change—and then click in the music to set the Play From point. Do the same with the right control to set the Play To point. Either control can be dragged when already present in the music. To return either control to its default position at the beginning or end of the piece, first click on the tool and then click anywhere to the left of the staff.

Spacebar

Use the spacebar to stop any music that's playing (it will also clear all current notes when using Harmony Keys).

Tools of the Music Window

• Each staff will have its handle at its left, which can be clicked with the mouse and dragged up or down. Clicking in the staff handle is also one way to activate a staff, as described above (the other is to click on any symbol in the staff). Just to the left of the staff handle is the staff sound switch. Turn off the sound for one or more staves if you want to hear only one voice in a multipart composition.

• To the left of the staff sound switch is the staff channel selector, which is visible only if the chosen output is via MIDI or QuickTime or a built-in synthesizer. Click on the number to change the output channel.

• To the left of the channel selector is the staff instrument name, which will be in the form of an icon if you are using sampled sounds. Click on the instrument name or icon to change the instrument assigned to that staff. If using MIDI, QT, or Synth, this will also change the output channel and instrument of the live keyboard.

• Above the staff handles is a small box that can be dragged downward to add extra space at the top of the first page of a printed piece of music.

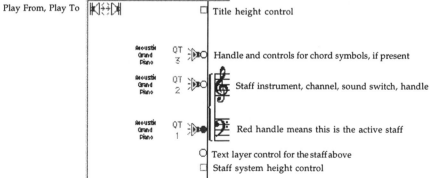

• Another box below the staves can be dragged up and down to adjust the amount of space between staff systems in a printed score. If your activity involves printing out a score, you may want to do a page preview to see the effect of this control.

Tools of the Screen Piano

Few Practica Musica activities will display all the tools at once, but they are all visible in the below illustration for the purpose of explanation. The buttons at the top of the piano will vary depending on the activity; and sometimes the tools will be replaced by a collection of multiple-choice boxes.

The type of keyboard can be changed in the Options menu; the selections include a fretboard, an "enharmonic" piano with 31 different note-names in the octave, and different types of labeled pianos.

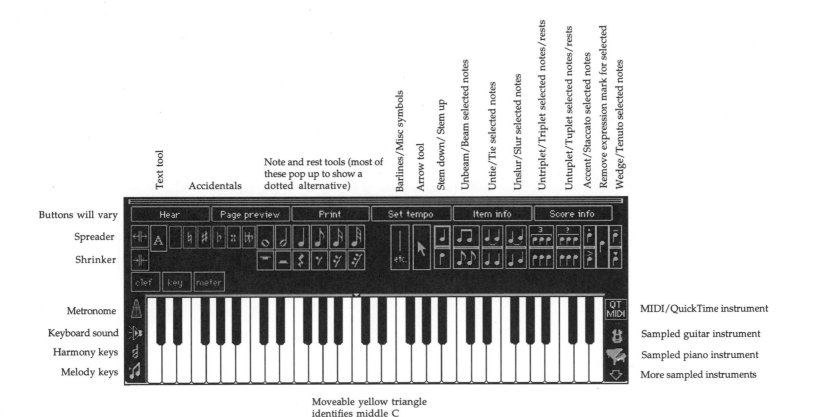

Moveable yellow triangle
identifies middle C

Keyboard Equivalents and Shortcuts

Whenever instructions refer to the Command key, we mean the Macintosh's Apple Key or the Ctrl key in Windows. Whenever we refer to the Option key, this will mean the Option key in Macintosh and the Alt key in Windows.

<u>Command keys</u>

Hold down the Command (Cntl) key and press the indicated letter key for these shortcuts:

Command-A: Select All.
Command-B: Beam selected notes.
Command-C: Copy selected items.
Command-G: Merge contents of another staff with the active staff.
Command-H: Hear the current music.
Command-K: Bring the Keyboard forward or send it behind.
Command-M: Toggle the metronome.
Command-N: New music window.
Command-O: Open a music file.
Command-P: Print music of current window.
Command-Q: Quit the program, or the current activity if you are in one.
Command-S: Save the music of current window.
Command-W: Close the current music window (when appropriate).
Command-T: Change the tempo.
Command-U: Toggle the Repeat function (music will repeat until you press Spacebar).

<u>Shortcuts not requiring the command key:</u>

Spacebar stops a play and/or clears current notes when using harmony keys.

Number keys 1-6. These are shortcuts for choosing note values when writing music. Once the cursor has been changed to a note by clicking on a note tool box, its value can be changed by pressing a number. 1 = whole note or rest. 2 = half note or rest. 3 = quarter note or rest. 4 = sixteenth note or rest. 5 = thirty-second note or rest. 6 = sixty-fourth note or rest. Holding Shift as you press the number adds a dot to the note or rest. Holding Option (Alt) as you press the number changes the note tool to a rest, or vice-versa.

"<" and ">" in the lower row of letter keys will lower and raise the pitch of the letter keys piano and screen piano, by octaves.

Textbook Activities

Textbook activities are found in Practica Musica's Textbook Activities folder, and are opened in the same way as any Practica Musica activity, by selecting the activity name in the Activity menu. If you would like the Textbook Activities to be the only ones appearing in the Activity menu, use the Change Activity Folder command, open one of the Textbook Activities, and then Save Settings to make that the default activity folder.

Examples, Ch. 1-5
Examples, Ch. 6-9
Examples, Ch. 10-13
Class Music

page

Index

Worksheet 1. Material: Chapter 1.

_____

name

A. Treble clef. Identify the pitches by name.

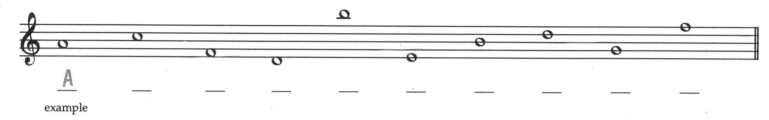

A

example

B. Bass clef. Identify the pitches by name.

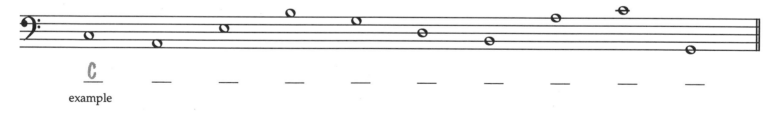

C

example

Worksheet 2. Material: Chapter 1.

name

A. Write the pitches as whole notes.

D   B   E   F   G   A   D   C   B   E

example

B. Using ledger lines, write these pitches above the staff.

C   B   E   A   D   C   E   G   F   D

example

C. Using ledger lines, write these pitches below the staff.

C   B   A   G   D   C   A   B   D   G

example

D. Write the appropriate clef for each note.

example

D   B   A   E   F   B

Worksheet 3. Material: Chapter 1.

_____
name

A. Write the following notes in the bass clef.

example

B. Write the name of the pitch. Then, without using ledgers, write a whole note that is either an octave above or an octave below it.

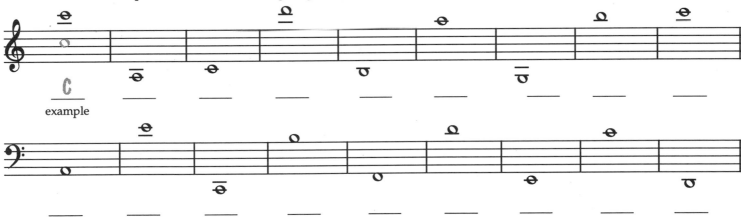

example

C. Using ledger lines when necessary, write whole notes an octave above and an octave below the given ones.

example

Worksheet 4. Material: Chapter 1.

name _____

A. Identify the intervals as whole steps (W) or half steps (H).

W
___
example

___ ___ ___ ___ ___ ___ ___ ___ ___

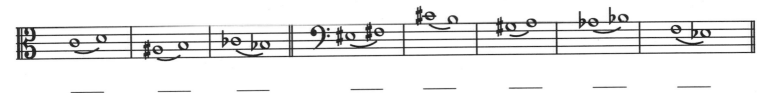

___ ___ ___ ___ ___ ___ ___ ___

B. Fill in the missing diatonic half step for each of these major scales. Each example begins on the tonic of the scale.

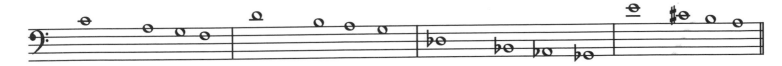

example

Worksheet 5. Material: Chapter 1.

_____
name

A. Write the lower half step of the requested type before each note, and the upper half step of the same type following it.

diatonic   chromatic   diatonic   chromatic

diatonic   chromatic   diatonic   chromatic

B. Write the lower diatonic whole step before each note, and the upper diatonic whole step following it.

example

Worksheet 6. Material: Chapter 1.

name _____

A. Write the requested pitches as whole notes.

example

C   F   G   D   B   E   A   C   F   G   D   B   E   A

B. Write the given pitches in the other clef.

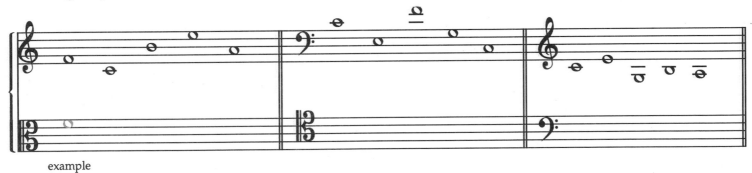

example

Worksheet 7. Material: Chapter 2.

name _____

A. Add stems to complete these half and quarter notes.   B. Add stems and beams to complete these pairs of eighth notes.

example   example

C. Add stems and beams to complete these groups of sixteenth notes.   D. Complete with stems and beams

example   example

E. Add a single note that completes each of these measures.

example

Worksheet 10. Material: Chapters 2 - 4

name _____

Add the missing barlines.

example

Worksheet 11. Material: Chapters 2 - 4

name _____

Add the missing barlines.

Worksheet 12. Material: Chapters 2 - 4

name

Rewrite each rhythmic pattern, correcting the beaming in accordance with the meter and adding ties where necessary.
Use downward stems for your corrected version, as in the example. Your corrected version will sound the same as the original, but
the metric organization of each measure will be easier to read.

example

Worksheet 13. Materials: Chapter 5.

name

Write a whole note at the requested interval *above* the given note.

example							
M3	m3	P4	M3	P5	M6	M7	m3

P4	m2	M2	m3	P5	M6	m6	m7

P5	M2	P8	P4	m6	M3	M7	m2

P5	m6	m3	M2	M7	M3	M6	P4

Worksheet 14. Material: Chapter 5.

name _____

Write a whole note at the requested interval *below* the given note.

example
P4   M3   M6   m6   P5   M2   m7   M7

m2   m6   M6   m7   P4   P5   M7   M3

P5   P4   M7   m6   M6   m2   m3   P8

P5   M7   m6   M7   P4   M3   m7   P4

Worksheet 15. Material: Chapter 5.

name _____

Write a whole note at the requested interval *above* the given note.

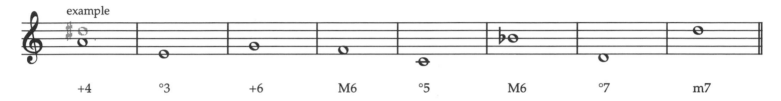

| +4 | °3 | +6 | M6 | °5 | M6 | °7 | m7 |

| +2 | m6 | +6 | °3 | °4 | °7 | M7 | M2 |

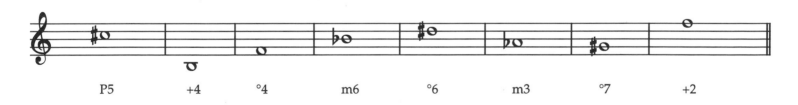

| P5 | +4 | °4 | m6 | °6 | m3 | °7 | +2 |

| P5 | M7 | °3 | M2 | P4 | °5 | m2 | +4 |

Worksheet 17. Material: Chapter 5.

name _____

Write in the other staff a compound version of the requested interval from the given note (compound = plus one or more octaves).

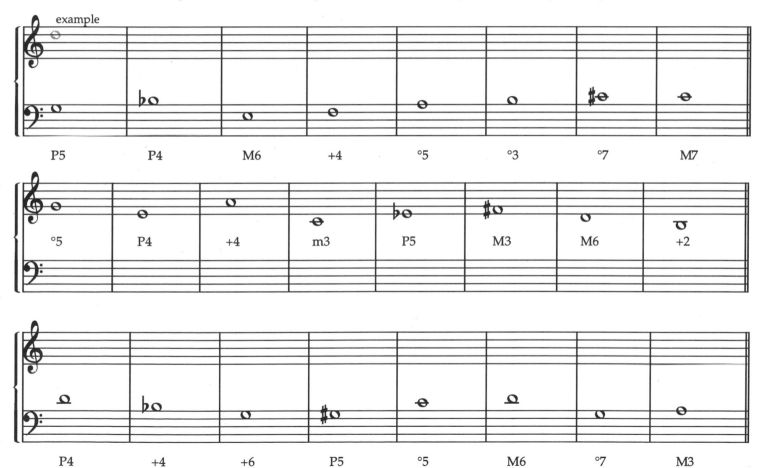

example

P5   P4   M6   +4   °5   °3   °7   M7

°5   P4   +4   m3   P5   M3   M6   +2

P4   +4   +6   P5   °5   M6   °7   M3

Worksheet 18. Material: Chapters 1,5.

_____
name

A. In each measure write another note that is the enharmonic equivalent of the given one.

B. In each measure write two notes that form a harmonic interval that is enharmonically equivalent to the given one.
Then identify both intervals by name.

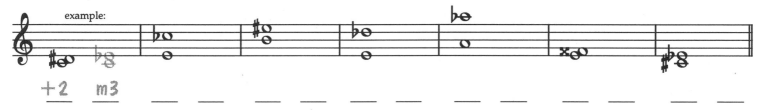

C. In each measure write the pair of eighth notes again, and change the second note of each pair to an enharmonic equivalent.
Then identify both intervals by name.

Worksheet 19. Material: Chapter 6.

name _____

Write the tonic notes for the major and minor keys represented by these signatures, major first.

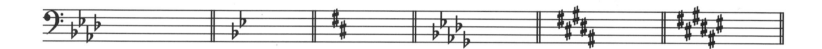

Worksheet 20. Material: Chapter 6.

name

Write the key signature for the major key whose tonic is the given note, and then the key signature for the parallel minor.

example

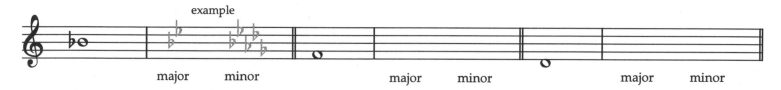

major   minor   major   minor   major   minor

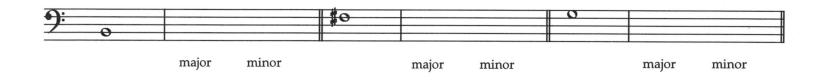

major   minor   major   minor   major   minor

major   minor   major   minor   major   minor

major   minor   major   minor   major   minor

Worksheet 21. Material: Chapter 6.

name _____

Provide the correct key signature at the beginning of each line and write each scale in ascending form, using quarter notes.

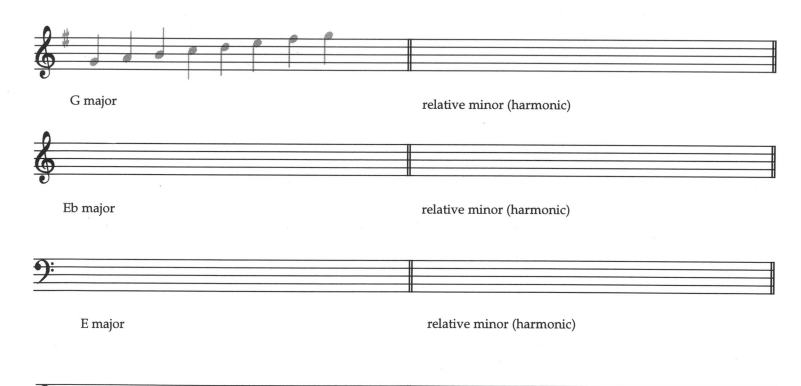

G major   relative minor (harmonic)

Eb major   relative minor (harmonic)

E major   relative minor (harmonic)

Db major   relative minor (harmonic)

Worksheet 22. Material: Chapter 6.

_____
name

Provide the correct key signature at the beginning of each line and write each scale in ascending form, using quarter notes.

g (harmonic) minor   relative major

b (harmonic) minor   relative major

f (harmonic) minor   relative major

g# (harmonic) minor   relative major

Worksheet 23. **Material: Chapter 7.**

_____
name

Provide the needed key signatures for each scale and write the scale in ascending form in quarter notes.

example

relative minor (harmonic) of G major   parallel minor (harmonic) of G major

relative minor (harmonic) of B major   parallel minor (harmonic) of B major

relative minor (harmonic) of Ab major   parallel minor (harmonic) of Ab major

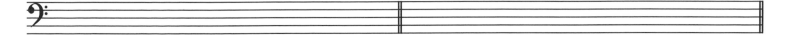

relative minor (harmonic) of A major   parallel minor (harmonic) of A major

Worksheet 24. Material: Chapter 7.

_____

name

Provide the needed key signatures and write the indicated scales in quarter notes, both ascending and descending.

example

g natural minor   g harmonic minor

f# natural minor   f# melodic minor

c natural minor   c melodic minor

g# natural minor   g# harmonic minor

Worksheet 25. Material: Chapter 7.

_____

name

Using quarter notes, write a root position triad of the requested type on each of these roots.

Mark all accidentals (for the sake of the exercise, assume that each accidental applies only to the note it precedes).

example

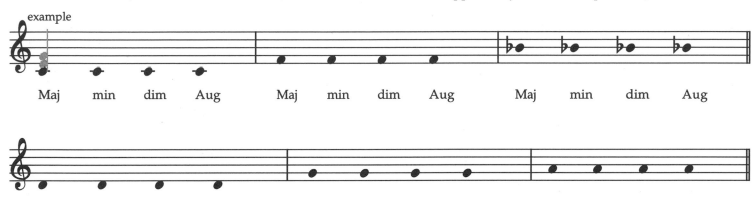

| Maj | min | dim | Aug | Maj | min | dim | Aug | Maj | min | dim | Aug |

| Maj | min | dim | Aug | Maj | min | dim | Aug | Maj | min | dim | Aug |

| Maj | min | dim | Aug | Maj | min | dim | Aug | Maj | min | dim | Aug |

| Maj | min | dim | Aug | Maj | min | dim | Aug | Maj | min | dim | Aug |

Worksheet 26. Material: Chapter 7.

name _____

Using half notes, write a root position triad of the requested type on each of these roots.

example

Maj   min   min   dim   min   Aug   dim   Maj

min   Maj   Aug   dim   Maj   Aug   dim   min

dim   Maj   Aug   min   min   Maj   dim   Aug

Maj   min   min   Maj   Aug   dim   dim   Aug

Worksheet 27. Material: Chapter 7.

_____
name

A. Name the chord (root and quality) and then rewrite it in first inversion, close position.

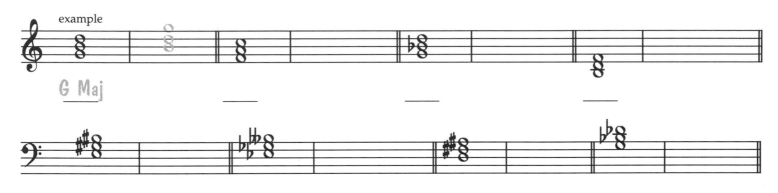

G Maj

_____   _____   _____

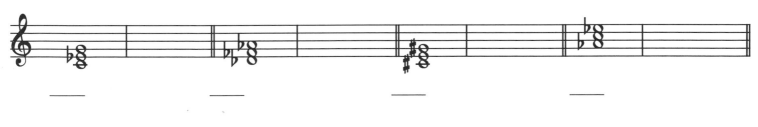

_____   _____   _____   _____

B. Name the chord (root and quality) and then rewrite it in second inversion, close position.

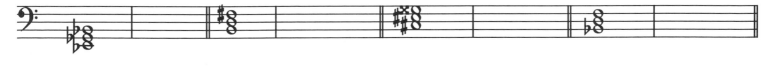

_____   _____   _____   _____

_____   _____   _____   _____

Worksheet 28. Material: Chapter 7.

_____
name

A. Write the primary triads for each of these major keys. Use close root position.

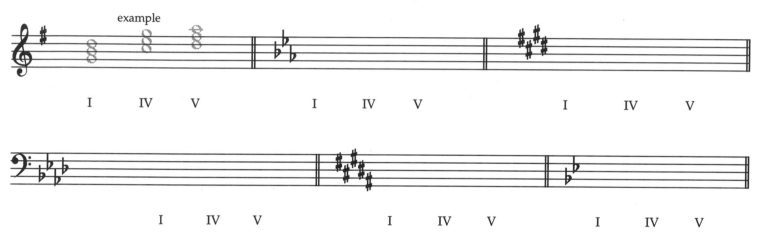

B. Again using close root position, write the primary triads for each of these minor keys. Remember to make V a major triad.

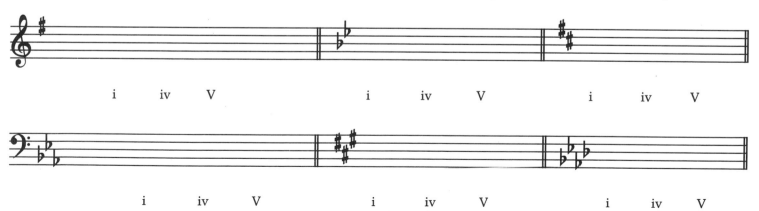

Worksheet 29. Material: Chapter 7.

_____

name

A. Using quarter notes, write the indicated secondary triads for each of these major keys in close root position.

B. Do the same for each of these minor keys, using the *harmonic* form of the minor scale.

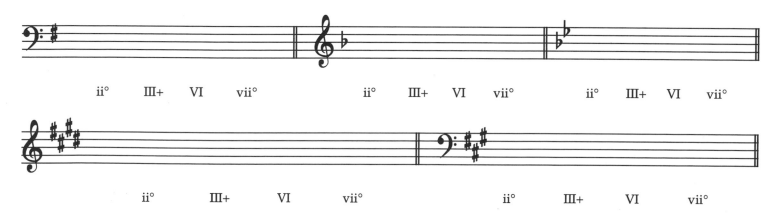

Worksheet 30. Material: Chapter 8

name

Write seventh chords of the requested type on each of these roots. Use close root position.

example

M7   dom7   m7   half-dim7   dim7   M7   dom7   m7   half-dim7   dim7

M7   dom7   m7   half-dim7   dim7   M7   dom7   m7   half-dim7   dim7

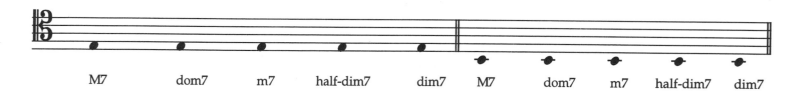

M7   dom7   m7   half-dim7   dim7   M7   dom7   m7   half-dim7   dim7

M7   dom7   m7   half-dim7   dim7   M7   dom7   m7   half-dim7   dim7

Worksheet 31. Material: Chapter 9.

name _____

Label the provided root position seventh chord as a minor 7th (m7) or a dominant 7th (dom 7) and then write the chord in the positions suggested by the figured bass symbols. Accidentals can be marked just at their first appearance in each measure.

Worksheet 34. Material: Chapters 10-11.

Write melodies using the following rhythms. You can use either the major or minor scales for the given key signatures.

Worksheet 35. Material: Chapter 11.

_____

name

Transpose the model melodies by the given amount and include the appropriate key signature.

Worksheet 36. Material: Chapter 11.

Transpose the model melodies by the given amount and include the appropriate key signature.

Transpose downward (real) a major second:

Transpose downward (real) a major sixth:

Transpose upward (real) a perfect fourth:

Transpose downward (real) a perfect fifth:

Worksheet 37. Material: Chapters 10-11.

Worksheet 37. Material: Chapters 10-11.

name

A. Write the given motives again, transposed tonally upward a second.

B. Write the tonal inversion of each motive.

C. Write the retrograde of each motive, keeping the rhythm of the original.

D. Write the retrograde inversion of each motive, keeping the rhythm of the original.

Worksheet 38. Material: Chapter 13.

_____
name

Realize the following harmonies in four parts, observing voice-leading principles. The bass line is provided.
If you would like to work on this using Practica Musica, which makes it easier for non-keyboard players to hear their work, you will find a textbook activity titled "Worksheet 38" that is set up with these examples in score; arranged one part per staff for easy editing.
When satisfied with your work, copy it by hand into this page.

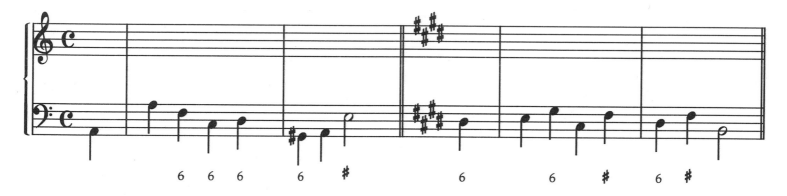

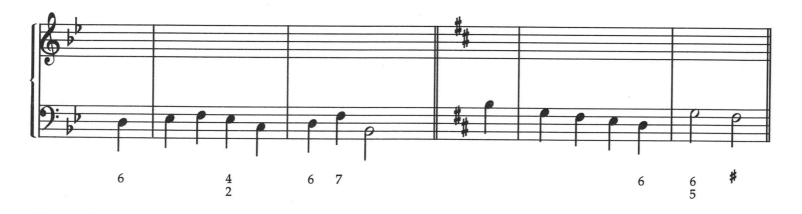

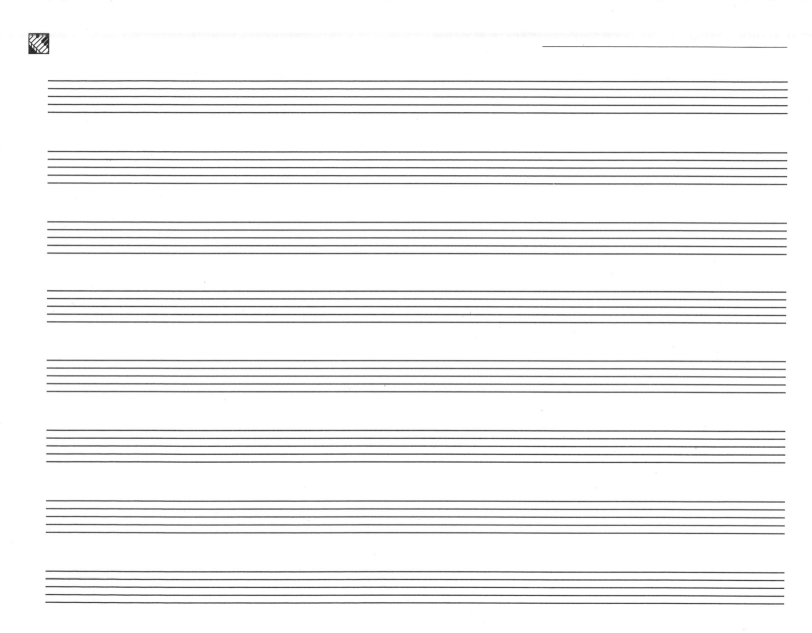

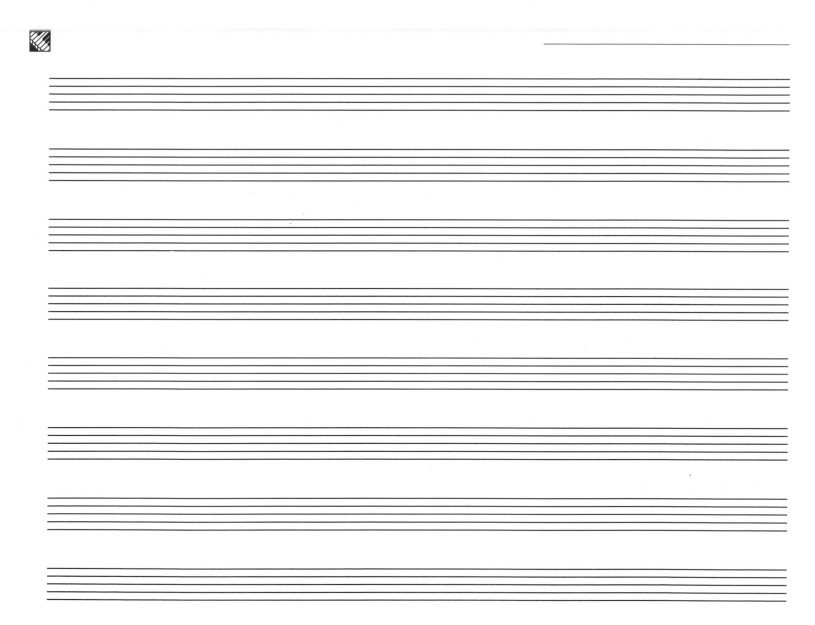